The
FREEMASONS

The
FREEMASONS

Unlocking the 1000-year-old mysteries of the Brotherhood:
the Masonic rituals, codes, signs and symbols explained
with over 200 photographs and illustrations

Jeremy Harwood

HERMES
HOUSE

This edition is published by Hermes House

Hermes House is an imprint of Anness Publishing Ltd
Hermes House, 88–89 Blackfriars Road,
London SE1 8HA

tel. 020 7401 2077; fax 020 7633 9499; info@anness.com

© Anness Publishing Ltd 2006

Designed and produced for Anness Publishing by
THE BRIDGEWATER BOOK COMPANY LTD.

Publisher Joanna Lorenz
Editorial Director Helen Sudell
Editor Sarah Doughty
Designer Barbara Zuñiga
Art Director Michael Whitehead
Editorial Readers Rosanna Fairhead, Jay Thundercliffe
Production Controller Wendy Lawson

10 9 8 7 6 5 4 3 2 1

PICTURE ACKNOWLEGEMENTS

Anness Publishing would like to thank the following for kindly supplying
photographs for this book: 1 Fidelity Masonic Supplies: 2 Grand British Lodge
of Columbia: 3 The Stapleton Collection (STC): 4 l STC, c STC: 5 t STC,
br STC, bl STC: 6–7 tl, r STC: 8 tl STC, bl Bridgeman Art Library (BAL):
9 tl STC, tr Grand British Lodge of Columbia: 10 tl BAL, b STC: 11 tl STC,
tr BAL: 12–13 tl, r STC: 13 STC: 14 tl STC, c STC, bl STC: 15 tr Tim
Wallace-Murphy, tl Tim Wallace-Murphy, br STC: 16 tl BAL, bl BAL: 17 tL
STC, tr STC, br STC: 18 tl STC, tr Grand British Lodge of Columbia, bl BAL:
19 tr STC, br STC: 20 tl STC, br STC, bl STC: 21 tl STC, tr STC, c Coral
Mula, br STC: 22 tl STC, bl STC: 23 tl STC, tr, STC, bl STC: 24 tl STC,
b STC: 25 t STC, tr STC, bl STC: 26 tl BAL, b STC: 27 t BAL, br STC: 28 tl
STC, br STC, l Grand British Lodge of Columbia: 29 t Grand British Lodge of
Columbia, tr STC, b STC: 30 tl BAL, b BAL: 31 tL STC, tr STC, br STC: 32–3
tl, r BAL: 34 tl STC, br STC, bl STC: 35 tl STC, tr © 2005 JupiterImages
Corporation: 36 tl STC, b STC: 37 tl STC, br STC: 38 tl STC, bl STC: 39 t
STC, br STC, b STC: 40 tl STC, br STC, l STC: 41 tl STC, tr STC, br STC:
42 tl STC, b Library and Museum of Freemasonry: 43 tl STC,
r STC, br BAL: 44 tl STC, b BAL: 45 tr BAL, br Grand British Lodge of
Columbia: 46 tl STC, bl STC: 47 t STC, br STC: 48–49 tl, r BAL: 50 tl STC, c
STC, lc STC: 51 r STC, bl STC, bl STC: 52 t STC, b STC: 53 tr STC, b STC:
54 tl STC, b STC: 55 tl STC, br STC: 56 tl STC, l STC: 57 t Fidelity Masonic
Supplies, b STC: 58 tl Grand British Lodge of Columbia, bl Grand British Lodge
of Columbia: 59 tr STC, br STC: 60 tl STC, cr STC, cl STC,
br Grand British Lodge of Columbia, bl STC: 61 t STC, br STC: 62 Grand
British Lodge of Columbia, cr STC, cl STC: 63 t STC, br Grand British Lodge
of Columbia: 64 tl STC, cl STC, b STC: 65 t STC: 66 Fidelity Masonic
Supplies, bl STC: 67 tl STC, tr Fidelity Masonic Supplies: 68 tl Fidelity Masonic
Supplies, c STC, bl Fidelity Masonic Supplies: 69 tr STC, br Grand British
Lodge of Columbia, bl STC: 70 tl Fidelity Masonic Supplies, r STC,
l Grand British Lodge of Columbia: 71 tl STC, r Fidelity Masonic Supplies:
72 tl BAL, bl Library and Museum of Freemasonry: 73 t STC, r STC, b BAL:
74 tl Grand British Lodge of Columbia, b Grand British Lodge of Columbia:
75 c Grand British Lodge of Columbia, r STC: 76 tl STC, b STC: 77 tr STC:
78 tl BAL, b Grand British Lodge of Columbia: 79 BAL: 80 tl Grand British
Lodge of Columbia, bl Grand British Lodge of Columbia: 81 tl STC, r Grand
British Lodge of Columbia: 82 tl STC, c Grand British Lodge of Columbia,
bc STC, bl STC: 83 t STC, cr Coral Mula, b STC: 84 tl STC, br STC, bc STC,
bl STC: 85 t Grand British Lodge of Columbia, br STC, bc STC, bl STC: 86 tl
STC, c STC: 87 tl Coral Mula, tr STC, br STC: 88 tl BAL, bl BAL: 89 tr BAL,
br Grand British Lodge of Columbia, bl Grand British Lodge of Columbia:
90 tl Fidelity Masonic Supplies, bl Grand British Lodge of Columbia: 91 tl
Fidelity Masonic Supplies, c Fidelity Masonic Supplies, r Fidelity Masonic
Supplies, bl STC: 92 tr STC, Grand British Lodge of Columbia, bl STC: 93 tr
STC, br STC, bl Tim Wallace-Murphy: 94 c STC, bl STC: 95 tl STC, c STC, br
STC: 96 tr STC, c STC, bl STC: Front flap top The Stapleton Collection
(STC), centre Grand British Lodge of Columbia, front cover and back cover left
to right top, The Stapleton Collection (STC), below Fidelity Masonic Supplies,
back flap top STC.

Every effort has been made to obtain permission to reproduce copyright material,
but there may be cases where we have been unable to trace a copyright holder. The
publisher will be happy to correct any omissions in future printings.

Images are listed in clockwise order from the top (t = top, c = centre,
b = bottom, r = right, l = left, tr = top right etc.)

CONTENTS

PART ONE

INTRODUCING FREEMASONRY

Freemasonry is the oldest and largest fraternal organization in the world. Put at its simplest, it is a universal society of friends who seek to become better people through their association with one another. Its watchwords are fellowship, integrity and good citizenship. Its origins, however, are obscure. Some trace the beginning of Freemasonry to the master masons who created the great churches and cathedrals of medieval Europe; some argue that its birth was linked to the Knights Templar, a military and religious order of warrior-knights who rose to prominence at the time of the Crusades. Others say that Freemasonry's roots go further back than that — to the time of King Solomon and the building of his great temple in Jerusalem, if not before.

RIGHT A fifteenth-century woodcut depicting the Old Testament story of building the Tower of Babel. The enterprise was believed to have been planned by Masons.

IDEAS AND IDEALS

FREEMASONRY IS NOT A RELIGION, THOUGH MANY CHRISTIAN IDEAS AND IDEALS ARE IMPORTANT TO
MASONS. IT IS WHAT MASONS TERM A FRATERNAL ORDER, WHOSE BASIC TENETS ARE BROTHERLY
LOVE AND RELIEF. BROTHERLY LOVE REQUIRES THAT MASONS BE TOLERANT, RESPECTFUL, KIND AND
UNDERSTANDING. RELIEF REFERS TO THE ACTIVE PRACTICE OF CHARITY AND COMMITMENT TO OTHER
FORMS OF PHILANTHROPY, AND TRUTH. THE ESSENTIAL QUALIFICATION ALL MASONS MUST SHARE IS
A BELIEF IN A SINGLE SUPREME BEING. MEMBERSHIP, THEREFORE, IS OPEN TO PEOPLE OF ANY RACE OR
RELIGION WHO CAN FULFIL THIS QUALIFICATION AND ARE "OF GOOD CHARACTER AND REPUTE".

BELOW The values of
Freemasonry personified
in a French lithograph. It
symbolizes the belief that
self-improvement paves
the way to enlightenment.

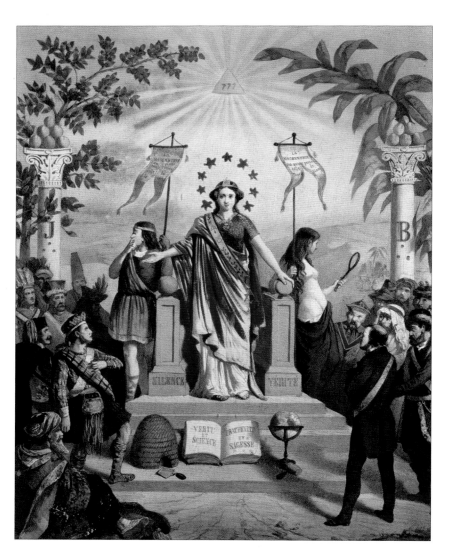

Being a Freemason means possessing a belief
that there is a divine intelligence that governs the
working of the universe. Freemasonry has no
doctrines or dogmas as such, or any political or
religious affiliations. Rather, it is a system of
morality, which is veiled heavily in allegory and
illustrated by symbols, with implications for a
way of living that leads to self-improvement
through service to the world. The Masonic
argument is that these are the surest ways by
which moral and ethical truths may be taught.
It is compatible with various world-views and
religious and philosophical traditions without
being limited to any one of them.

THE GROWTH OF MASONIC RITUAL

Much of the ritual that surrounds Freemasonry
has grown up over the centuries. To the uninitiated
many of the rituals appear to have come from
obscure traditions. It is evident, for instance,
that Freemasonry relies heavily on notions
gleaned from the customs and practices of the
stonemasons of medieval times. It is undoubtedly
from stonemasonry that the Square and the
Compasses – two of the best known of
all Masonic symbols – derive. Together with the
Bible, these make up the three Great Lights of
Freemasonry in Christian countries. Elsewhere,
the appropriate volume of Sacred Law replaces
the Bible.

Arguably, the most important of the Square's
many meanings – with its immovable legs set at
90° – is that it represents matter. The Compasses,

MASONRY AND THE CHURCH

The Masonic ideals of truthfulness, toleration and the nobility of the human soul are completely in accordance with the tenets of Christianity and other world religions. This has not stopped Freemasonry from being attacked by religious organizations, however – notably by the Roman Catholic Church, which condemned it as basically irreligious.

which have movable adjustable legs, represent consciousness or spirit. Both are regularly shown in combination, suggesting that matter and consciousness are interdependent realities.

FROM MYTHOLOGY TO PRACTICE

Freemasonry revolves around the creation of an all-embracing central mythology. This mythology features heavily the building of King Solomon's Temple in Jerusalem as its central theme. Some Masons go even further than this view, suggesting that Freemasonry has highly charged symbolic links with other similar initiatory orders throughout human history – and sees itself as the chief modern form of the Ancient Mysteries.

In practice, Freemasonry operates on a number of levels – a fact recognized in the various degrees that members of a lodge have to pass through as they progress in Masonic knowledge. The overriding truth is that when you become a Mason, you commit yourself to exploring a unique design for living. Under the guidance that Freemasonry can provide, eventually you will reach the gateway that marks the beginning of the great journey along the path of self-discovery. By following this path to its logical conclusion, you will end up with a revelatory knowledge of your inner nature and understand the way in which you link harmoniously with all other life on the planet.

ABOVE In this illustration, Truth uses her mirror to light up Freemason's Hall, London. Companion figures symbolize faith, hope and charity.

ABOVE LEFT God Almighty, as depicted in the Cathedral of the Assumption, Moscow. Belief in the existence of a Supreme Being of any faith lies at the heart of Freemasonry.

ORIGINS AND ALLEGORIES

SOME FREEMASONS CLAIMED THAT THE ROOTS OF THE SOCIETY, IN COMMON WITH OTHER MYSTIC TRADITIONS, LIE FAR BACK IN ANCIENT EGYPT AND BIBLICAL ISRAEL. BUT MOST MASONIC SCHOLARS TODAY ACCEPT THAT THERE IS NO FIRM EVIDENCE FOR SUCH LINKS. THEY BELIEVE THAT FREEMASONRY IN ITS ORIGINAL FORM EVOLVED FROM THE MEDIEVAL STONEMASONS' GUILDS, OR THAT IT CAME ABOUT AS A RESULT OF A DISPERSAL OF KNOWLEDGE FOLLOWING THE SUPPRESSION OF THE QUASI-RELIGIOUS MILITARY ORDER KNOWN AS THE KNIGHTS TEMPLAR. WHATEVER THE TRUTH, CLEARLY FREEMASONRY DERIVES ITS RITES AND RITUALS FROM VARIOUS SOURCES — SOME MORE ARCANE THAN OTHERS.

BELOW The sacrifice of the Israelites on the site that was to become Jerusalem, where King Solomon's Temple was built. The tabernacle, housing the Ark of the Covenant, is depicted in the background.

It seems highly unlikely that the true origins of Freemasonry will ever be uncovered. The majority of Masons believe that the modern story of the movement began with the stonemasons, builders of Europe's greatest cathedrals. Member masons were craftsmen, who banded together to practise what Masons today call "the operative art" of masonry. They were an elite class that could travel freely between countries — unlike serfs, whose movements were carefully controlled and closely restricted. Hence, the term "free mason" came into being.

LEFT Rosslyn Chapel, Scotland, is thought to be modelled on Herod's Temple, and Knights Templar are said to have had a hand in its building.

FAR LEFT The Apprentice's Pillar in Rosslyn Chapel was supposedly the work of the Master Mason's apprentice. He was killed by his master in a fit of jealous rage at the perfection of the construction.

it is known that this was not the case. There is further evidence to support the Scottish link – the connection between Templars and Masons in Rosslyn Chapel, a few miles south of Edinburgh. Sir William St Clair built the chapel in 1440 to house artefacts originally brought to Scotland by the Knights Templar in 1126.

It has been suggested that the chapel was built as a replica of Herod's Temple in Jerusalem, which the Templars had excavated during their time in the Holy Land. Even more importantly, the chapel contains a unique carving, which some scholars are certain depicts the initiation of a Mason by a figure wearing a Knight Templar's mantle.

Unfortunately, what is lacking is indisputable historical proof. Although the link is disputed by many scholars, it is entirely possible that fugitive Templars were admitted into the fraternities of Scottish stonemasons.

THE ROSSLYN CONNECTION

Rosslyn Chapel's unique stone carvings makes it important in the story of Scottish Freemasonry. One of the carvings depicts the chapel's Master Mason, who, in an act resembling the murder of Hiram Abif (the architect of King Solomon's Temple) is said to have killed his apprentice in a fit of jealous rage following the latter's creation of the so called Apprentice's Pillar. This pillar is a representation of the Norse Tree of Knowledge, the Christian equivalent of which is the Tree of Life.

LEFT A Masonic Scottish badge of uncertain date celebrates the supposed link between early Freemasonry and the Knights Templar. The belief is that refugee Templars joined Scottish Operative Lodges.

LEGEND AND RITUAL

FOR FREEMASONS, LEGEND IS EXTREMELY IMPORTANT, ESPECIALLY WHEN IT COMES TO THE PRACTICE OF THE RITES, RITUALS AND MYSTERIES OF THE CRAFT. KING SOLOMON'S TEMPLE IS IMPORTANT BECAUSE MASONS SEE IT AS THE PRIME EXAMPLE OF DIVINE ARCHITECTURE. LINKS WITH ANCIENT EGYPT ARE ALSO CLAIMED. THERE ARE CLEAR PARALLELS BETWEEN THE LEGEND OF HIRAM ABIF, WHICH IS ANOTHER CENTRAL FEATURE IN MASONIC RITUAL, AND THE MUCH OLDER ONE OF ISIS AND OSIRIS. GREEK LEGEND, TOO, PLAYS ITS PART, NOT SURPRISINGLY SINCE MATHEMATICS, AND MORE SPECIFICALLY GEOMETRY, IS ANOTHER KEY MASONIC THEME.

BELOW An Apron worn by a French eighteenth-century Master Mason. Note in particular the two columns, symbolizing Boaz and Jachin (as seen from the perspective of the Temple), the Temple itself, and the group of Masonic emblems in the foreground.

THE LEGEND OF THE PILLARS

Pillars play a conspicuous part in Masonic ceremonies, the most significant of them being the two named pillars – Boaz and Jachin. According to Masonic legend, the original pillars were erected at the entrance to King Solomon's Temple, Boaz on the left of the porchway and Jachin on the right. Their purpose, it has been claimed, was to give divine legitimacy to the ruling dynasty; in Hebrew, Jachin means "for God will establish", while Boaz is a composite of two words, "bo" meaning "in him" and "az" meaning strength. The pillars were thus a testament to the power and might of God.

The pillars were cast of bronze. It is likely that they stood at least 3m/10ft tall. They were hollow – though the theory that they were used to house secret archives has long been discounted – and adorned with capitals in the shape of huge bowls, each 2m/7ft deep.

The bowls were ornately rimmed with two rows of pomegranates, while lily work also featured. Both have their own meaning in Freemasonry – the pomegranate symbolizes plenty, while the lily stands for the need for modesty and rectitude. The significance of Boaz in Freemasonry is revealed during First Degree initiation rites; that of Jachin during the rituals that mark the passage from First to Second Degree.

THE OLD CHARGES

The manuscripts and other documents collectively known as the Old Charges are also an important feature of the legendary traditions of Freemasonry. Masons regard knowledge of their contents as essential for an understanding of Masonic constitutional law and practice.

LEFT Pages from the Regius (far left) and Cook (left) manuscripts. They date from the end of the fourteenth and early fifteenth centuries and, together with other early documents, make up what Masons call the Old Charges.

The Old Charges all originated in England. The earliest – the Regius Manuscript and the Cook Manuscript – date from around 1390 and 1420 respectively. It is likely that the Cook Manuscript is the more authentic, since internal evidence suggests that a practising Mason wrote it. The bulk of the documents date from the late sixteenth to the early eighteenth centuries, starting with the Grand Lodge No. 1 Manuscript of December 1583. Historians have queried the authenticity of later documents, often regarded as antiquarian curiosities. The Regius Manuscript is in verse, the others in prose; apart from this difference, all have a more or less identical form. They start with an opening prayer, followed by a detailed history of Freemasonry, tracing its origins back to the days before the Flood and charting its growth and spread through the ages until its establishment in England in Saxon times. This is followed by a code of regulations for Master Masons, Fellow Masons and Apprentices, covering craft practices and morals, arrangements for large-scale assemblies, procedures for the trial and punishment of offenders and admissions procedures for "new men that were never charged before", including an oath of loyalty.

THE 'WILLIAM WATSON MS.', A.D. 1687

LEFT An extract from the "William Watson manuscript". This may be another important Masonic document, but historians query the authencity of some of the later records of Freemasonry. This manuscript is believed to be dated around 1687.

THE LEGEND OF ENOCH

How, when, why and where Freemasonry originated is a legend in its own right. It can be traced back to the time of Enoch, the seventh of the Hebrew patriarchs of the Old Testament and the great-grandfather of Noah. He is said to have initiated and promoted a Craft in which the eternal truths of Freemasonry were revealed through emblems, symbols, mystics and mysteries.

THE HIRAMIC LEGEND

THE LEGEND OF HIRAM ABIF, THE MASTER ARCHITECT OF KING SOLOMON'S TEMPLE, IS ONE OF THE CENTRAL ALLEGORIES IN FREEMASONRY. HIS MURDER AT THE HANDS OF THREE OF HIS SUBORDINATE CRAFTSMEN FOR REFUSING TO REVEAL THE SECRETS OF MASTER MASONRY, AND HIS SUBSEQUENT REBIRTH, DESCRIBED AS HIS RISE FROM "A DEAD LEVEL" TO "A LIVING PERPENDICULAR", IS A KEY PART OF THE RITUAL THAT MARKS THE PROGRESS OF A MASON FROM THE SECOND TO THE THIRD DEGREE.

BELOW A depiction of the death of Hiram Abif, King Solomon's master architect, murdered by his underlings for refusing to divulge the most hidden of Masonic secrets.

The story is as follows. Each day at noon – High Twelve, in Masonic parlance – Hiram Abif went into the temple to pray. Three of his subordinate craftsmen, who aspired to become Master Masons, lay in wait for him one day as he came out, their plan being to force him to reveal the secret words of recognition. Upon his refusal, each of them attacked Abif in turn. Finally, he fell to the ground, dead. The murderers buried their victim, but a search party led by Solomon himself found the grave. Then, after Entered Apprentices and Fellow Craftsmen had failed to resurrect their master, Solomon, a fellow Master Mason, raised him with the "strong grip of a lion's paw".

The legend became part of Freemasonry between 1723 and 1738. It is clearly not history – it is a ritualistic drama, actually acted out in the lodge during the process of Third Degree initiation, in which the candidate plays the part of Hiram Abif. Through their participation in the ritual, candidates learn how the soul can rise above its internal enemies – ignorance, lust, passion and sin – so that they can become masters of themselves and their destinies.

THE MYSTERIES

According to the great Masonic scholar Albert Mackey, the legend of Hiram Abif was borrowed from what scholars term the Ancient Mysteries of early Egypt, Mesopotamia and Rome. This is described in Dr Albert G. Mackey's *Manual of the Lodge*, in which he argues that there is no biblical evidence that such a character ever existed and met his death in such a way. Rather than being part of any biblical tradition, Abif is the representative of the gods Osiris, Baal and Bacchus.

RIGHT A ceremonial sword of a type used in the initiation of a Master Mason. It is ornately detailed with symbolic emblems along much of the length of the blade.

BELOW Acting out the murder of Hiram Abif is central to the rituals governing admission to the Third Degree.

BOTTOM The candidate is raised after a symbolic death, where his face is covered and swords are pointed at his body.

This is by no means the only supposed link with the Ancient Mysteries. It is argued that the Compasses and Square, for instance, represent ancient pagan sun deities, while, like the sun temples of the ancient Middle East, Masonic temples are usually built on an east–west axis. Venturing slightly further ahead in time, Masonic writers have often claimed to see many resemblances between Freemasonry and Mithraism, the cult of the Persian god Mithras that eventually spread from its homeland to the Roman Empire itself.

The existence of direct and arcane links between Freemasonry and the Ancient Mysteries is disputed by many present-day Masons. While they admit there are similarities between their fraternity and the old mystery cults – just like Freemasonry, Mithraism featured elaborate initiation rites for its various successive degrees – Masons point out that most of the similarities are superficial in character. In the main, Masons are concerned with the externals of rite or organization rather than deeper content.

MITHRAISM AND MASONRY

Nineteenth-century Masonic writer Albert Pike declared that Freemasonry was "the modern heir" of the Ancient Mysteries, and Sir Samuel Dill described Mithraism as "a sacred Freemasonry". There are certainly similarities. Like Freemasonry, Mithraism was divided into grades, each of which had its own symbolic ceremonies to mark initiation. As in Masonry, the practice of charity was important, while, like Masons, Mithraists greeted one another with the word "brother".

CLASSICAL LEGENDS

EGYPT HAS ALWAYS BEEN CONSIDERED TO BE THE BIRTHPLACE OF THE MYSTERIES. IT WAS IN EGYPT THAT CEREMONIES OF INITIATION WERE FIRST ESTABLISHED, TRUTH WAS FIRST VERSED IN ALLEGORY, AND THE DOGMAS OF RELIGION WERE FIRST IMPARTED IN SYMBOLIC FORMS. SOME BELIEVE THAT THE LEGEND OF HIRAM ABIF IS BASED ON THE SUPPOSED FATE OF THE EGYPTIAN GOD OSIRIS. THOTH, THE ANCIENT EGYPTIAN GOD OF WISDOM, PLAYED A MAJOR PART IN PRESERVING THE KNOWLEDGE OF THE MASONS' CRAFT AND TRANSMITTING IT TO FUTURE GENERATIONS. GREECE HAS ALSO BEEN ASSOCIATED WITH SYMBOLISM – THROUGH THE ANCIENT ELEUSINIAN MYSTERIES AND GREEK FIGURES SUCH AS PYTHAGORAS.

BELOW The tombs of the kings outside Thebes demonstrate how important hieroglyphs were in ancient Egypt. Freemasonry borrowed from such traditions.

BELOW RIGHT According to some Masonic scholars, Isis, the Egyptian goddess of fertility, and her husband Osiris are linked to the origins of Freemasonry.

LEARNING FROM THE EGYPTIANS

Much of Masonic architecture and formal dress – notably the Masonic Apron – is indebted to ancient Egyptian precedents. Unfortunately, no amount of research has yet been able to establish any causal link between the two. We do know, however, that in ancient Egypt the architects and craftsmen who worked on that civilization's monumental building projects, such as the pyramids, were accorded a special status in contemporary society. Additionally, they were organized into guilds. Evidence for this comes from papyrus records, one of which describes a guild that held secret meetings in around 2000BC. Its members met to discuss working conditions, wages and rules for daily labour. They also provided charitable relief to workers' widows and orphans, and to workers in distress. The parallel between the kind of organizational duties described in the papyrus and those of a Warden or Master in a Freemasons' lodge is strong. However, this may be nothing more than coincidence, and it is unlikely that anyone will ever be able to establish the truth.

LEARNING FROM THE GREEKS

Just as they looked towards ancient Egypt, some Freemasons historically thought that the culture and civilization of ancient Greece contributed to the development of Masonic rites and ritual. The ancient Eleusinian Mysteries — so called because they were celebrated at Eleusis, near Athens — have parallels with the Masonic commemoration of Hiram Abif's martyrdom, but, again, this is probably no more than coincidental.

One major Greek figure traditionally associated with Freemasonry is undoubtedly Pythagoras, an Ionian Greek who was probably born in around 570BC on the island of Samos and rose to become one of the most celebrated mathematicians of all time. He founded his own secret society, the Pythagoreans, among whom the pentagram, or five-pointed star, was a symbol of health and knowledge. The sign also became associated with rites of initiation, just as it is in Masonic iconography — often appearing on Masonic

regalia, such as the jewels of office worn by the Masters of Lodges and Grand Masters of Grand Lodges, and in decorative illustration. One reason for its appearance may be that it can be interpreted as a representation of the Golden Ratio, knowledge of which is vital for all architects and builders.

Some Masons believe another Greek figure is linked to Freemasonry's origins: the inventor-craftsman Daedalus, who designed the Cretan labyrinth for King Minos to house the legendary Minotaur. Daedalus is said to be the inventor of a number of the tools used in the various degrees of Freemasonry — notably the plumb line — while Perdix, his nephew, is the reputed inventor of the compasses, Freemasonry's third Great Light.

THE ELEUSINIAN MYSTERIES

Of all the mysteries celebrated in ancient times, the Eleusinian ones were considered to be the greatest in importance. They were basically initiation ceremonies for the cult of Demeter, the Greek goddess of life, agriculture and fertility, and Persephone, her daughter. The mysteries celebrated Persephone's reunion with her mother after Hades, the god of the underworld, had kidnapped her.

ABOVE The labyrinth built by Daedalus for King Minos of Crete. Some Masons think that Daedalus was an early proponent of the Craft.

ABOVE LEFT The Sphinx and the Great Pyramid were built by skilled craftsmen who may have been proto-Masons.

ABOVE In Greek legend Daedalus and his son, Icarus, flee Minoan Crete. Icarus paid with his life when he ignored his father's advice and flew too close to the sun. The wax that held his wings together melted and he fell from the skies.

THE RENAISSANCE

WITH THE COMING OF THE RENAISSANCE, WESTERN EUROPEAN SOCIETY WENT THROUGH A SERIES OF RADICAL CHANGES. IN AROUND 1450, A PLATONIC ACADEMY WAS FOUNDED IN FLORENCE – AND IN 1471 A LATIN TRANSLATION OF THE RECENTLY REDISCOVERED GREEK *CORPUS HERMETICUM* APPEARED. IT WAS TO PROVE IMMENSELY INFLUENTIAL. FREEMASONRY HAD ALREADY RECOGNIZED THE IMPORTANCE OF ANCIENT KNOWLEDGE. IT NOW SHARED IN THE HERMETIC QUEST FOR LOST WISDOMS.

Like many other thinkers, the Masons dreamed of greater freedom of thought, and political and religious reform. Given the climate of the times, when many governments and the Catholic Church fiercely opposed such radical thinking, it was hardly surprising that its activities now came to be conducted in secrecy.

The nature of Freemasonry itself went through a transformation during this turbulent period. The impetus for this came from Scotland, where in 1583 King James VI and I appointed Sir William Schaw, a Scottish nobleman with a passionate interest in architecture, as Master of the Work and Warden General. In 1598 Schaw issued the first of the celebrated statutes which set out the duties that Masons owed to their lodges. The second statute, issued in 1599, is the first Masonic document that had survived to make veiled reference to the existence of esoteric knowledge within the Craft. The new spirit of the Renaissance was obviously having its impact, enabling Schaw to revive and develop medieval Masonic mythology and rituals. In Scotland, Freemasonry appeared to have royal backing. According to William Preston in his *Illustrations of Masonry* (1772), James became "the patron of the learned and zealous encourager of Masonry".

LEFT James VI and I depicted with his wife Anne of Denmark. James was a staunch supporter of Freemasonry.

Scottish records relate that "he honoured the lodges with his royal presence" and that "he settled a yearly revenue of four pounds Scots to be paid by every Master Mason to a Grand Master chosen by the Grand Lodge and approved by the Crown". James was also the first king known to be a Freemason and was initiated into the Lodge of Scots and Perth in 1601 at the age of 35.

The earliest known record of a Masonic initiation anywhere is that of John Boswell, the Laird of Auchenleck, who was initiated into the Lodge of Edinburgh in June the preceding year.

Thus the scene was set for the further transformation of Freemasonry that was to gather momentum during the seventeenth century, though just how or when the transition from Operative Masonry to Intellectual Masonry took place is not clear. We do know, however, that as the guild system began to break down, what is known as Operative Masonry started to evolve into what is termed Speculative Masonry. Eventually the operative side was to be lost altogether with Masons being drawn chiefly from the nobility and the rising bourgeoisie.

ABOVE A seventeenth-century notion of an astrologer's costume. The beginnings of modern science were closely linked with those of Speculative Freemasonry.

ABOVE LEFT A letter from Sir William Schaw, Master of Work to James VI and I. A Mason himself, Schaw played a leading part in organizing and expanding Scottish Freemasonry.

LEFT The notion of ideal proportions became an important Masonic principle.

SCIENCE AND ALCHEMY

THE SEVENTEENTH CENTURY WAS A TIME OF GREAT POLITICAL UPHEAVAL AND SOCIAL CHANGE. IN BRITAIN CHARLES I WAS BEHEADED; ON THE EUROPEAN CONTINENT, BITTER RELIGIOUS WAR WAGED FOR 30 YEARS. FREEMASONRY GREW APACE, CLOSELY LINKED TO THE EMERGENCE OF A NEW GENERATION OF SCIENTISTS AND SAVANTS, WHO BECAME ASSOCIATED WITH THE MOVEMENT AS IT EXPANDED. MASONRY BECAME SO FASHIONABLE THAT, AS THE CENTURY PROGRESSED, ACCEPTANCE MEMBERS (THE COLLECTIVE TERM FOR NON-OPERATIVE MASONS) BECAME THE MAJORITY IN MANY MASONIC LODGES.

BELOW Astronomers search the heavens for stars and planets. Many of the emerging generation of new scientists were Freemasons.

Scientists such as Robert Boyle, Christopher Wren and Isaac Newton were all early members of the Royal Society, which had begun life as a quasi-Masonic institution called the Invisible College. In its early years, the Royal Society often held meetings in the Compton Room at Canonbury Tower in north London. The room is decorated with carvings of Masonic significance. They were commissioned by Francis Bacon, a Mason and one of the Invisible College's founder leaders. A champion of inductive reasoning, Bacon has often been described as "the father of modern science".

In its early days, the proceedings of the Invisible College were cloaked in secrecy, as these were times of fear, state control and relative intolerance. Galileo, one of its founders, was condemned by the Catholic Church for daring to suggest that the earth revolved around the sun. Personal safety probably demanded that discussion of anything of an esoteric, moral or scientific nature took place underground. It seems more than probable that those seeking a vehicle in which they could discuss what the outside world might regard as dangerous ideas and beliefs freely would turn to Freemasonry. What emerged as a result was a new Speculative form of the Craft, which merely bore an allegorical likeness to the earlier Operative traditions.

OLD BELIEFS, NEW SCIENCE

Past beliefs intermingled with the new as much in science as in Freemasonry. Elias Ashmole, who was one of the first recorded inductees into English Freemasonry, was initiated as a Mason in Warrington, Lancashire, in 1646. He was a founder member of the Royal Society and stands as a good example of how old arcane beliefs and the new science could coexist. In 1652 Ashmole published his *Theatrum Chemicum Britannicum*, a compilation of all the writings on alchemy that had been produced by English authors, including those of Dr John Dee, the great Elizabethan savant and reputed magician. It should not be forgotten that, at this time, men of science still believed in the possibility of the transmutation of base metals into gold, the notion of a possible Elixir of Life, and other arcane beliefs. Newton himself spent a great deal of time trying to calculate the date of the end of the world.

For Freemasonry, the branch of science of greatest interest was undoubtedly geometry. Knowledge of geometry was an essential part of the Masonic tradition. Masons now came to believe that such knowledge would make it possible to recognize the principles upon which nature and society were built.

LEFT An alchemist's laboratory. The search for the Philosopher's Stone and the Elixir of Life were part of a quest for knowledge that fitted in well with the most important of Masonic principles.

ABOVE Lawyer and philosopher Sir Francis Bacon was James VI and I's Lord Chancellor and a leading light of the Invisible College. This was the precursor of the Royal Society.

LEFT Alchemy, with its arcane beliefs, slowly transmuted into modern chemistry. Freemasons were interested in all the new sciences, most notably that of geometry.

WAS SIR FRANCIS BACON A FREEMASON?

Though many have claimed that Sir Francis Bacon was a Freemason, there is no hard historical evidence to show that he was ever formally initiated into the Brotherhood. What is known is that he actively encouraged the setting up of the Mason's Hall in London as the model for an allegorical "Solomon's House", the inspiration for which came from Bacon's celebrated tract *The New Atlantis*.

AGE OF ENLIGHTENMENT

THE EIGHTEENTH CENTURY MARKED MAJOR NEW BEGINNINGS FOR FREEMASONRY. FOUR LODGES BANDED TOGETHER IN 1721 TO FORM THE PREMIER GRAND LODGE IN LONDON. IN 1731 THE GRAND LODGE OF PENNSYLVANIA, THE FIRST GRAND LODGE TO BE FOUNDED IN WHAT WOULD LATER BECOME THE USA, OBTAINED ITS CONSTITUTION; BY THE END OF THAT DECADE, THERE WERE LODGES IN BELGIUM, RUSSIA, ITALY, GERMANY AND SWITZERLAND. FIVE LODGES WERE FOUNDED IN PARIS BY 1742.

BELOW A seventeenth-century illustration records humanity's progress in the sciences, including those of geometry and architecture. Both are central to Masonic thinking.

Freemasonry stood for rationalism, deism and benevolence – three of the most important characteristics of the Enlightenment ideas and ideals that were swiftly coming to prominence. What differed was the way in which these ideals were interpreted and applied. According to Michael Baigant and Richard Leigh's *The Temple and the Lodge*, as early as the 1730s, Freemasonry in England was fast becoming a pillar of the social

and cultural establishment. It fostered a spirit of moderation, tolerance and flexibility, and often worked hand in hand with the established church. Many clergymen became Freemasons themselves. There was a major rift within Freemasonry in 1751, however, when the so called Ancients broke away from the Moderns of the existing Grand Lodge. The former were so called because they believed that they adhered more faithfully to

L'ACADEMIE DES SCIENCES ET DES BEAUX ARTS
DEDIE'E AU ROY.
. Par son tres humble, tres obeïssant et tres . fidèle Serviteur et sujet Seb. le Clerc.

traditional Masonic ritual, passwords and customs. The breach between the Ancients and Moderns was not healed until 1813, when the United Grand Lodge of England was formed.

In Catholic Europe, on the other hand, Freemasonry just as quickly became identified with militant anticlerical, anti-establishment and eventually revolutionary ideas. In France, for instance, prominent Freemasons, such as the Marquis de Lafayette, Georges Danton and Emmanuel-Joseph Sieyès, were prime movers in the overthrow of the Bourbon monarchy in the Revolution of 1789. These leaders believed they were acting in full accordance with Masonic ideals.

THE AMERICAN REVOLUTION

It is likely that the first native-born American to be made a Mason was Jonathan Belcher, the governor of Massachusetts, in 1703, and the Order soon grew in power and influence. Freemasons played a significant part in the events leading up to the Declaration of Independence and the subsequent struggle to free the American colonies from British rule. William Bramley in *The Gods of Eden* claims that a Masonic lodge – St Andrew's Lodge in Boston – was the prime mover in the Boston Tea Party of 1773, for instance, while Michael Baigent et al. in *The Messianic Legacy* argues that most of the men responsible for creating the USA "were staunch Freemasons" and that "the new nation was originally conceived as the ideal hierarchic political structure postulated by certain Masonic rites".

What is known for a fact is that of the five men appointed by the Continental Congress to draft the Declaration of Independence, two were Masons, as were 19 signatories of the Declaration itself. They included George Washington, Benjamin Franklin and John Hancock, the president of the Congress. Franklin was Provincial Grand Master of Philadelphia and visited lodges in England, Scotland and France. He was the American publisher of the *Constitutions of the Freemasons,* which had been drawn up in the 1720s.

ABOVE The composer Mozart (seated extreme left) at a Viennese initiation ceremony.

BELOW George Washington, founding father of the United States, was an active Mason for most of his life.

MASONIC RITUAL

IT WAS IN THE 1720S, SHORTLY AFTER THE FOUNDING OF THE FIRST GRAND LODGE IN ENGLAND, THAT THE MASONIC RITUAL OF INITIATION WAS CLARIFIED INTO A SYSTEM BASED ON THREE DEGREES, OR LEVELS. IN THE EARLY DAYS OF FREEMASONRY, THERE HAD BEEN ONLY TWO DEGREES. NOW A THIRD ONE WAS ADDED, FOLLOWED LATER BY THE ROYAL ARCH DEGREE. IN BLUE LODGE MASONRY, THE PROCESS ENDS THERE. HOWEVER, ANY MASTER MASON (SOMEONE WHO HAS BEEN INITIATED INTO THE THIRD DEGREE) IS ELIGIBLE TO JOIN THE YORK RITE, WHICH HAS NINE FURTHER DEGREES, OR SCOTTISH RITE (UP TO 32 DEGREES). A 33RD DEGREE MASON OF THE SCOTTISH RITE IS AN HONORARY POSITION.

THE FIRST DEGREE

Of the Three Degrees, the first is that of an Entered Apprentice. The initiation begins when the "hoodwinked" (blindfolded) and specially dressed candidate is brought before the entrance to the inner part of the temple and a guard hits the door with his sword hilt. After questions as to his eligibility and whether his motives are "worthy", and a short prayer, he is led three times around the meeting room, pausing on each lap to be introduced as "a poor candidate in a state of darkness". He is then brought before the Worshipful Master's pedestal (the Worshipful Master is the leader of the lodge) where he is asked: "What is the predominant wish of your heart?" The answer —"Light"— is whispered to

ABOVE Candidates for the First and Second Degrees of Freemasonry learn the significance of the pillars Boaz and Jachin during their respective initiation rituals.

RIGHT Masons assemble to initiate an Entered Apprentice. In this eighteenth-century depiction the Master of the Lodge is questioning the candidate before he reveals the secrets of the First Degree to him.

him and the blindfold removed. The Three Lights – the volume of Sacred Law (such as the Bible), the Square and the Compasses – are then revealed, followed by an explanation of the secret signs, grips and passwords of the First Degree and the meaning of Boaz, the left-hand pillar in King Solomon's Temple. It ends with the presentation of a Masonic Apron to the initiated candidate.

THE SECOND AND THIRD DEGREES

The Second Degree is that of Fellow Craft Mason. The candidate is admitted to the temple just as he was during his First Degree initiation, following which he has to recite answers to a number of questions that he has memorized. Among other things, these introduce him to "the hidden mysteries of science and nature", which he is now expected to study. He is again led around the temple, new signs and passwords are explained, and he learns the meaning of Jachin, the right-hand pillar of King Solomon's Temple.

The Third Degree – "the cement of the whole" according to the ritual – is that of Master Mason. Having answered more test questions successfully, the candidate enters the temple, which is in pitch darkness. After a prayer and a ceremony that resembles those of the first two degrees, the Worshipful Master and his fellow Masons act out the story of Hiram Abif, with the initiate playing the part of Hiram and his fellow Masons his murderers. It is the Worshipful Master who eventually raises the candidate to his feet, after which the initiate kneels before the altar and, resting his hands on the Three Lights, takes the Master Mason's oath.

MASONIC MONITORS

To help to understand rituals, many Masons rely on small books called Monitors, which explain the meanings of the major Masonic symbols and the important parts of the ritual itself.

PAST INTO PRESENT

IN SOME WAYS, THE NINETEENTH CENTURY WAS A HIGH WATERMARK FOR FREEMASONRY, YET IT ALSO CONTAINED THE SEEDS OF A PARTIAL DECLINE. IN EUROPE THERE WERE FURTHER SPLITS IN THE MOVEMENT, NOTABLY BETWEEN THE FRENCH FREEMASONS AND THEIR ENGLISH AND AMERICAN CONTEMPORARIES FROM 1877 ONWARDS. THE CHIEF REASON FOR THE RIFT WAS THE DECISION OF THE FRENCH GRAND LODGE OF THE ORIENT TO START ACCEPTING ATHEISTS AS INITIATES. THE FRENCH RECOGNITION OF WOMEN'S MASONRY ADDED FUEL TO THE FLAMES, AS DID THE WILLINGNESS OF FRENCH FREEMASONRY TO BECOME ACTIVELY INVOLVED IN MAJOR POLITICAL AND RELIGIOUS ISSUES.

BELOW Initiating a woman into Freemasonry in France in the mid-nineteenth century. The introduction of this practice led to a split between French Freemasonry and Masonry as practised in England and Scotland which has never been healed.

There was also the growth of anti-Masonic feeling to consider. In the USA, this began during the 1820s and led to the foundation of the Anti-Masonic Party in 1827. The party even fielded its own candidate for president against Andrew Jackson, who himself was a Mason. The growth of such feelings led to a change in Masonic thinking and direction. In response to

political and religious criticism, American Masonry turned inward, emphasizing spiritual values as opposed to its earlier, more public espousal of Enlightenment ideas. The lodge became a sanctuary that men could repair to for solace and inspiration.

Anti-Masonic feelings were not confined to the USA – in Catholic Europe they were just

LEFT Ornately carved and decorated columns line the approaches to the inner regions of the Grand Temple on the island of Philae, one of the great temples of the ancient Egyptians. They worshipped the sun and the sun god. Freemasons seek the inner light and spiritual enlightenment.

BELOW Cleopatra's Needle in New York is an obelisk with a pyramid as its apex. Both were Egyptian architectural inventions and both play important symbolic roles within Freemasonry.

were Masons, and soon they had set to work digging and excavating. Among their discoveries was the Rosetta Stone, which eventually provided the key to the deciphering of hieroglyphs.

As far as French Freemasonry was concerned, the interest in ancient Egypt, which so gripped the public at large as a consequence of the Napoleonic invasion, actually predated that event. Some years before in Paris, the mysterious Count Alessandro Cagliostro had founded the Egyptian Rite of Freemasonry, based upon Egyptian magic and masonry, which attracted many members of the French nobility into its ranks. He also claimed to be an agent of the Order of the Knights Templar and to have received initiation from them on the island of Malta. Today, Cagliostro is almost universally condemned as a charlatan and as an adventurer, but at the time his teachings had considerable impact. According to Manly P. Hall in *Rosicrucian and Masonic Origins*, when the Supreme Council of the Grand Orient called Cagliostro before them to justify his founding of an independent lodge, "they found it difficult to

secure an advocate qualified to discuss with Cagliostro philosophic Masonry and the Ancient Mysteries he claimed to represent".

Though the Egyptian Rite is no longer regarded as a legitimate Masonic ritual, there can be no doubting the impact it had on the Craft at the time and the stimulation it gave to the spread of Egyptian influence. This peaked in the nineteenth century, at a time when Masonic architecture as a whole was becoming more flamboyant and ornate.

In almost every Masonic lodge, there are representations of pyramids and sphinxes. When associated with the Eye of Providence, the pyramid is said to represent the Supreme Being, the Great Architect of the Universe. Another major Masonic symbol that was also important in Egyptian architecture is the obelisk, best described as a tall, vertical tower with a pyramid at its peak. In Freemasonry, obelisks are associated with the sun and various mythologized astronomical phenomena. They are symbols of continuity, power, stability, resurrection and immortality.

CLASSICAL ARCHITECTURE

IN *THE CONSTITUTIONS OF THE FREEMASONS*, ONE OF THE SEMINAL DOCUMENTS OF FREEMASONRY (FIRST PUBLISHED IN 1723), JAMES ANDERSON STATED UNEQUIVOCALLY THAT "THE ARTS OF BUILDING ATTAINED THEIR HIGHEST DEGREE OF PERFECTION UNDER THE ROMAN EMPEROR AUGUSTUS, WHO WAS THE PATRON OF VITRUVIUS". ANDERSON AND HIS FELLOWS EXPECTED MASONS TO SHARE THEIR ENTHUSIASM FOR THE ORDERED ARCHITECTURE OF THE CLASSICAL WORLD AND THEIR DETERMINATION TO USE THE PROCEDURES OF BUILDING TO ILLUSTRATE THE PROCESS OF SPIRITUAL DEVELOPMENT.

ABOVE An architectural representation of a classic pillar design. According to Masonic tradition, classical architecture derived its most important principles from King Solomon's Temple where Freemasonry was born.

RIGHT The five classical Orders of Architecture: from left to right, Tuscan, Doric, Ionian, Corinthian and Composite. Three of them – Corinthian, Doric, and Ionian – feature in Masonic architectural symbolism.

The ideas put forward by Marcus Vitruvius Pollio – to give the great Roman architect and engineer his full name – in his *De Architectura Libri Decem* (Ten Books on Architecture) were themselves encapsulations of the best and most important precepts of the classical architectural tradition. According to Masonic tradition, these precepts derived from the Temple of Solomon. Pythagoras brought the secrets of architecture, which were carved on the two pillars of the temple that play such important symbolic roles in Masonic ritual, back to Greece, from where they spread to the West. They were centred on the two cardinal ideals of order and simplicity. The Masons revere three of the classical architectural orders: Corinthian, Doric and Ionic. In Masonic architectural symbolism, Doric stands for strength, Ionic for wisdom and Corinthian for beauty.

BUILDING A TRADITION

Masonic thinking was also influenced by the Renaissance concept of the architect as the Universal Man, master of all the arts central to human knowledge. From the eighteenth century onwards, initiates could receive instruction in mathematics and listen to lectures on the new science at Masonic lodges. They became part of a fellowship that claimed to be descended from the earliest Masonic architects who constructed the ancient temples, and those who designed the

medieval cathedrals and practised the "Royal Art". One such eighteenth-century paragon was Batty Langley, a Freemason and an architect, who ran a building school in London. According to the prospectus, Langley taught "young Noblemen and Gentlemen to draw the Orders of Columns in

Architecture, to design Geometrical Plans and Elevations for Temples, Hermitages, Caves, Grottoes, Cascades, Theatres, and other Ornamental Buildings of Delight, to lay out and improve Parks and Gardens".

Possibly unconsciously, Langley was following one of Vitruvius' cardinal precepts. In *The Education of an Architect*, Vitruvius wrote that an architect "should be equipped with knowledge of many branches of study and varied kinds of learning, for it is by his judgement that all work done by the other arts is put to the test".

This was a view with which Freemasonry was quick to concur. The Craft approved wholeheartedly of the dominant Palladian style, which, taking its cue from the neo-classical work of the Italian architect Palladio, demanded that every great building conform to the orders of architecture that had been prescribed by the ancient Greeks. That legacy persists. In the rituals that accompany admission to the

Fellow Craft Degree, for instance, architecture features prominently, with elaborate descriptions and assessments of the importance of each of the classical orders.

ABOVE Frontispiece of an architectural study printed in Renaissance Venice. According to Renaissance thinking, architects were masters of all the arts central to knowledge. The parallel with Freemasonry and its beliefs is obvious.

ABOVE LEFT The column supporting the elaborate pediment in this drawing, signed by Batty and Thomas Langley, is Corinthian – a Masonic symbol of beauty.

LEFT Italian architect Andrea Palladio was the leader of the classical revival and, as such, was later revered by the new generation of Speculative Freemasons in the eighteenth century.

MASONIC BUILDINGS

LODGES AND TEMPLES HAVE NOT ALWAYS BEEN IMPOSING WORKS OF ARCHITECTURE. IN THE EARLY DAYS, FEW MASONIC LODGES HAD PREMISES OF THEIR OWN — THEY MET IN THE UPSTAIRS ROOMS OF TAVERNS AND COFFEE HOUSES. EVEN THE PREMIER GRAND LODGE OF ENGLAND DID NOT POSSESS A PERMANENT HOME UNTIL 1775 WHEN A HOUSE WAS PURCHASED IN GREAT QUEEN STREET.

BELOW Freemason's Tavern, Lincoln's Inn Fields, London, hosted the inaugural dinner of the Royal Astronomical Society in 1820. The event is clear evidence of Freemasonry's continuing links with speculative science.

The architecture of the lodge is particularly important for imparting the appropriate solemnity during Masonic ceremonies. There is also a commonality to the style of Masonic architecture, wherever it is found, and it exists in a time warp of its own devising. If a Mason of today could travel back in time to an eighteenth-century lodge, he would find many architectural similarities.

Masonic buildings are sometimes called temples, because much of the symbolism that Freemasonry uses to teach its lessons comes from the building of the Temple of King Solomon in the Holy Land. The term lodge comes from the structures that medieval Masons built against the sides of cathedrals during their construction. In winter, when work on the building had to stop, they lived in these lodges and worked at carving stone.

However, perhaps the most significant feature is the layout of the lodge itself. According to Masonic lore, this should ideally follow the supposed layout of King Solomon's Temple as closely as possible. It should have a porch with two pillars, a main sanctuary and an inner Holy of Holies. The two pillars, Jachin and Boaz, have in themselves considerable symbolic importance in Masonic ritual.

BACK TO THE EGYPTIANS

There was a further predominant influence on the architecture of lodge buildings – that of ancient Egypt. From the nineteenth century onwards, it became the norm for Masons to incorporate elements of Egyptian design into their buildings, just as Egyptian thought came to play a significant part in actual Masonic ritual. The 31st Degree of the Scottish Rite, as devised by noted nineteenth-century Masonic scholar Albert Pike, was based on the Book of the Dead (a record of ancient Egyptian mortuary spells) and includes references to the murder of the god Osiris and his resurrection.

The large windowless lodge room of the Silvergate Temple in San Diego, California, for example, was designed to be an exact replica of an Egyptian throne room, while in the Royal Arch Halls of the Chapter Room, Edinburgh, the use of Egyptian motifs extended to the furniture and carpets. The George Washington Masonic National Memorial in Virginia is a replica of the mighty Pharos of Alexandria, one of the original Seven Wonders of the Ancient World.

THE GRANDEST TEMPLE

The Masonic Temple in Detroit, which was dedicated in 1926, is still the largest and most complex building of its kind in the world. The 14-storey tower is Gothic in inspiration. There are seven Craft Lodge Rooms – all have different decorative treatments, inspired by Egyptian, Doric, Ionic, Corinthian, Italian Renaissance, Byzantine, Gothic and Romanesque motifs. The rooms are all faithful to the period.

ABOVE The Pharos of Alexandria was the inspiration for George Washington's Masonic Memorial in Virginia.

ABOVE LEFT Building the first pyramid at Giza. The use of skilled stonemakers could be interpreted as evidence of a link with the beginnings of Freemasonry.

BELOW A nineteenth-century French Master Mason's Apron. The main symbolic theme is architectural imagery.

THE LODGE INTERIOR

IN COMMON WITH OTHER RITUALISTIC SOCIETIES, FREEMASONRY PLACES ENORMOUS IMPORTANCE ON THE ARRANGEMENTS OF ITS MEETING PLACES. TO MASONS, THE LODGE REFERS BOTH TO A MEETING OF A GROUP OF MASONS AND TO THE ROOM OR BUILDING IN WHICH THE GATHERING TAKES PLACE. ONLY WHEN PURPOSE-BUILT LODGES AND TEMPLES BECAME THE NORM WERE MASONS ABLE TO SET OUT THEIR FURNITURE AND EQUIPMENT ON A MORE OR LESS PERMANENT BASIS, AND THE LAYOUT ITSELF BECAME AN IMPORTANT AND CONSTANT MASONIC SYMBOL.

BELOW A grand dinner in Freemason's Hall, London. The scene is an eloquent testament to the way Freemasonry has grown since the days of meetings in hired rooms above taverns and coffee houses.

Lodges conventionally take the form of oblong squares, though records show that some early ones seem to have been triangular and others cruciform. Generally, as far as Blue Lodge Freemasonry is concerned, the traditional English floor plan is followed. The Worshipful Master of the Lodge sits in the east, which Masonic lore associates with the sun, light and life. At the other end of the

lodge are three steps, one for the First Degree, one for the Second Degree and one for the Third. There is always an altar or table with the Volume of Sacred Law open on it if a lodge is meeting.

Because Masons consider protecting the secrets of their ceremonies to be so important, lodges usually lack windows. Instead, they are lit by candlelight. The candles themselves have their own

FAR LEFT A pyramid and the Eye feature on the dollar bill (Great Seal). Despite what anti-Masonic writers say, there is no evidence that Freemasonry inspired their presence.

LEFT The Eye of God watches over humanity. The symbol is not unique to Freemasonry; it often features in Christian art.

BELOW An elaborate invitation to Lodge meetings features the All-Seeing Eye, the Sun, the Moon and the two pillars of King Solomon's Temple. All are Masonic symbols.

Given the active and constant anti-Masonic propaganda, it seems highly unlikely that Freemasonry had anything to do with the Great Seal's origins. None of the designers of the Seal was a Mason. It seems likely that the misinterpretation of the Great Seal as a Masonic symbol started in 1884, when Eliot Charles Norton, a Harvard professor, wrote that the reverse "can hardly look otherwise than as a dull emblem of a Masonic fraternity". From that seemingly innocuous comment, an elaborate Masonic conspiracy theory grew, which is still accepted by many even today.

In fact, although Freemasonry may have eventually adopted the notion of the All-Seeing Eye, it is not a uniquely Masonic symbol at all. The eye inside an equilateral triangle, point up or point down, often appears in Christian art, while the depiction of a single eye was a well-established artistic convention for an "omniscient ubiquitous deity" in Renaissance times.

EYE OF HORUS

Known as the *indjat* or *wedjet* by the ancient Egyptians, the Eye of Horus was the symbol of the falcon-headed god Horus and Re, the Sun god. It was said to have healing and protective powers. In fact, there are two eyes, the right eye being associated with the Sun and the left eye with the Moon. The two eyes represent the balance between reason and intuition and light and dark.

Sun and Blazing Star

In Freemasonry, the sun and the moon together represent wisdom, power and goodness, while the Blazing Star is an emblem of divinity and of resurrection. This is not surprising, since one of the chief aims of the Craft is to guide its initiates along the path that leads to the true light. However, references in Masonic writings to these and other astronomical phenomena have led many to believe that Freemasonry is linked to astrology through its history, beliefs and practices. Nothing could be further from the truth.

RIGHT The earth, sun and moon feature on this Masonic medal.

FAR RIGHT Another Masonic medal highlights the Blazing Star.

BELOW A seventeenth-century astronomer. The study of the stars is an important feature of Freemasonry.

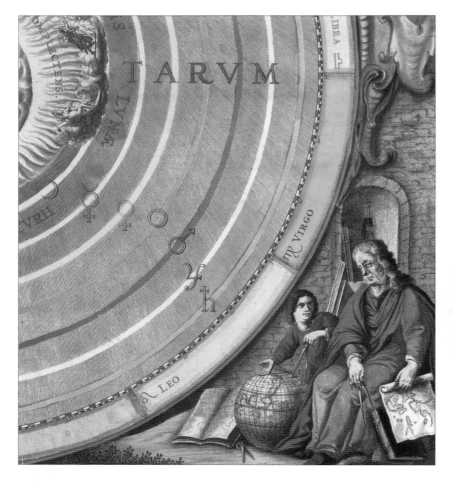

THE SUN

Ways of linking Freemasonry to the ancient and arcane rituals of sun worship started some time in the nineteenth century and have persisted up to the present day. In their 1977 book *The Hiram Key* for instance, Christopher Knight and Robert Lomas state: "Freemasons today claim always to meet symbolically at noon on the basis that Freemasonry is a worldwide organization and therefore the Sun is always at its meridian with respect to Freemasonry. Masonic reference to God as 'the most high' is therefore a description of Re, the sun god of the ancient Egyptians, in his ultimate position, the zenith of the heavens at noon." By the same token, attempts have been made to prove that some of the mystical words in Masonic ritual are "pure Egyptian". If anything, however, the origins of such words can be traced back to ancient Hebrew.

None the less, it is the case that there are links between the Craft and astronomy. As early as AD819, the Archbishop of Mainz wrote: "Astronomy teaches the laws of the stellar world, which is built up on the investigation of natural phenomena in order to determine the course of the sun, the moon, and the stars and to effect a proper reckoning of time." This is very close to what Masons believe.

THE BLAZING STAR

Similarly, anti-Masonic writers have made attempts to link the Blazing Star of Freemasonry with the worship of Venus and participation in occult rituals. This, too, is incorrect. Along with the Mosaic Pavement and Indented Tessel, the Blazing Star is one of the Ornaments of the Lodge and features briefly in the rituals that accompany admission to the First Degree.

The Blazing Star has a double symbolism, similar to that of the Indented Tessel, which is the border or skirting that surrounds the pavement. The first is straightforward – the star symbolizes the sun – but is of secondary importance. The star's prime purpose is to symbolize the Supreme Being, reminding us of "the omnipresence of the Almighty" and the fact that "wherever we may be assembled together, God is in the midst of us,

seeing our actions and observing the secret intents and desires of our hearts". The star is identified with the Star of Bethlehem that alerted the shepherds to the birth of Jesus and guided the Three Wise Men across the desert to the scene.

MASONS AND THE SUN

The sun is one of the Lesser Lights of Freemasonry. As a source of light, it is a reminder to Masons to strive for intellectual enlightenment. This is one of the reasons why all ceremonies in Freemasons' lodges are performed facing east. Masonic ritual proclaims that "as the sun rises in the east to open and govern the day, so rises the Worshipful Master in the east to open and govern his Lodge". Together with the moon, which governs and rules the night, the sun represents the active forces of nature, which must be in balance for the latter to exist.

ABOVE According to Masonic ritual, an understanding of the "laws of the stellar world" is vital "to effect a proper reckoning of time".

BELOW An Irish Masonic jewel from the late eighteenth century features the Blazing Star and other symbols.

THE MOON

IN MODERN MASONIC RITUAL, THE MOON IS THE SECOND OF THE LESSER LIGHTS OF FREEMASONRY. ITS PLACE IN THE MASONIC PANTHEON STEMS FIRST FROM THE BOOK OF GENESIS, IN WHICH IT IS RELATED HOW, ON THE FOURTH DAY OF CREATION, GOD "MADE TWO GREAT LIGHTS; THE GREATER LIGHT TO RULE THE DAY AND THE LESSER LIGHT TO RULE THE NIGHT". IT IS ALSO LINKED TO THE PRACTICE OF ALCHEMY IN MEDIEVAL TIMES, FOR IT WAS THE ALCHEMISTS WHO FIRST GAVE THE MOON A SYMBOLIC AND RITUALISTIC SIGNIFICANCE. FOR THEM IT STOOD FOR SILVER AND WAS USED TO DEPICT THAT METAL IN THEIR SECRET WRITINGS.

ABOVE LEFT To the alchemists, the moon was a symbol of the metal silver. To Freemasons, however, it is the second of the Lesser Lights of the lodge.

ABOVE RIGHT To the Freemasons, the moon is a symbol of regularity, associated with the way phases of the moon are used to measure the passage of time.

In alchemy, stylized drawings of the sun and the moon with human faces were among the most frequently used images. Early Masonic tracing boards utilized practically the same symbols, so it is clear that, in this respect at least, the first Speculative Freemasons owed a debt to their predecessors, even if there are no direct links between the Craft and that forerunner of modern science. Other images which are used in Freemasonry, such as depictions of the Plumb, Square, Level, Rough Ashlar and Perfect Ashlar, similarly made their first documented appearances in alchemical texts.

THE LESSER LIGHTS

References to the sun, moon and Master of the Lodge as the three Lesser Lights of Freemasonry appear to have originated in the so-called Antient Grand Lodge in England after the split with the original Premier Grand Lodge, which took place in the mid-eighteenth century. American Masonry, in particular, was quick to adopt the Antient interpretation.

In the First Degree initiation ceremony, the moon is identified as the biblical ruler of the night. In a more general symbolic context, it is also associated with the lodge's Senior Warden, who is positioned to the west of the lodge's Master during such rituals. According to some Masonic commentators, just as the moon's light is a reflection of that of the sun, the Senior Warden reflects the light of the lodge's Master. In this context, it is also significant that the Junior Deacon, who acts as the messenger of the Senior Warden within the lodge, wears the Square and Compasses, enclosing the moon as his Masonic jewel.

MOON LODGES

The moon has a practical as well as a symbolic relevance in Freemasonry although, perhaps paradoxically, this has only heightened the confusion that exists among many non-Masons as to its Masonic significance. Back in the early days of the Craft, it was literally a beacon that Masons could use to help them find the way home in the dark after lodge meetings, particularly in rural areas. Hence the practice grew up of holding lodge meetings during the week of the full moon. Such lodges became referred to as moon lodges.

ALCHEMY AND MASONRY

The alchemists were a group of mystics dating from around the twelfth century, and the forerunners of modern chemists. One of their key beliefs was that base metals, such as lead, could be turned into precious ones. But they were also philosophers who used symbols and drawings extensively in their teachings. Much of the graphic symbolism in Masonry, such as the images of the Plumb, Square, Level, Rough Ashlar and Perfect Ashlar, owe their existence to earlier alchemical texts and writings.

From this, it is easy to see how the notion of Masons as moon worshippers could have arisen. Now, however, the number of such lodges is in steep decline as the need for setting the date of meetings according to the phases of the moon rather than on fixed days has disappeared.

ABOVE Observing the phases of the moon. It was the medieval alchemists who gave the moon graphic and ritualistic importance.

BELOW A humanized moon surrounded by stars often features on Masonic Tracing Boards.

THE GLOBES

SIGNS AND SYMBOLS

THERE ARE TWO GLOBES ASSOCIATED WITH THE RITES OF THE CRAFT. MASONS BELIEVE THE ORIGINS OF THESE GLOBES COULD BE TRACED BACK TO THE TWIN COLUMNS THAT STOOD AT THE ENTRANCE TO KING SOLOMON'S TEMPLE, A GLOBE RESTING ON EACH. THE CELESTIAL GLOBE SYMBOLIZED THE SPIRITUAL PART OF HUMAN NATURE WHILE THE TERRESTRIAL GLOBE SYMBOLIZED THE MATERIAL SIDE. THEIR PRESENCE AT MASONIC LODGES TODAY EMPHASIZES THAT THE BELIEF IN FREEMASONRY IS UNIVERSAL.

According to the Masonic lecture traditionally delivered on the subject of the Second Tracing Board, there were "two great pillars that were placed in the porchway entrance on the south side…they were formed hollow, the better to serve as archives for Freemasonry, for therein were deposited the Constitutional Rolls…these pillars were adorned with two chapiters…with two spheres on which were delineated maps of the celestial and terrestrial globes, pointing out 'Masonry Universal'." It is a nice description but pure mythology.

Unfortunately, there is absolutely no proof that globes surmounted Solomon's columns – or, indeed, that they were hollow – though it is thought possible that they might have been decorated with bronze bowls, the precise purpose of which remains unknown. Indeed, there is not even a mention of the columns in the Old Charges, though Solomon and David, his father, are named as being among the people who "loved Masons well".

Globes were adopted as headpieces to the columns some time during the eighteenth century, but there is no evidence to show that they formed any part of the Masonic catechism or ritual before

ABOVE LEFT Tycho Brahe's system of planetary orbits. The first reference to astronomy in Freemasonry comes in the Cooke Manuscript, one of the Old Charges.

LEFT The situation of the earth in the heavens – another way of stressing the Craft's universality.

GLOBVS CŒLESTIS.

SPHÆRA ARMILLARIS
elevata supra Horizontem ad Latitudinem
Noribergensem.

GLOBVS TERRESTRIS.

SPHÆRA ARTIFICIALIS est instrumentum, seu structura quædam motum et dispositionem
Sphæræ Naturalis repræsentans. Illius partes, ex quibus constat, sunt Majores et Minores Circuli,
Lineæ rectæ, et Puncta. Majores Circuli sunt Horizon, Meridianus, duo Coluri, Æquator et Zodi-
acus. Minores circuli, duo Tropici, et duo Polares. Lineæ sunt, duo Axes, unus Polorum Mundi, alter
Zodiaci. Puncta denique nominantur, Centrum, Zenith et Nadir. plura, de hac re scire volentem
multo præstantior ipse materialium seu realium Globorum usus docebit.

around 1745. It was then, it seems, that spheres
or globes first started to appear in Masonic
floor drawings and on Tracing Boards. As far
as Solomon's columns are concerned, the first
records of globes appearing on them date from
the 1760s and 1770s.

Whenever it happened, the introduction of
the two globes came about slowly and was by no
means consistent. Sometimes, the globes stood
separately on four-legged or tripod stands to
the left and right of the Master of the Lodge's
pedestal. It seems that in many lodges, the
globes formed a part of lodge equipment in
their own right while in others, they found no
place at all.

GLOBES AND MAPS

It also seems likely that the tradition of globes
featuring celestial and terrestrial maps is late
eighteenth century rather than Biblical in origin.

In its 1775 edition, *The Illustrations of Masonry* deals
at some length with the nature of the globes, the
spiritual and moral lessons to be learned from
them, and the importance of astronomy in
Freemasonry, but it is not until 1802 that there
is any confirmation that maps appear on them
and that the latter have any part in Masonic
symbolism, allegory or ritual.

PRESTON AND THE GLOBES

It was William Preston in his *The Illustrations of
Masonry*, first published in 1775, who first made
detailed and specific reference to terrestrial and
celestial globes. He defined them as "the noblest
instruments for giving us the most distinct idea
of any problems or propositions, as well as for
enabling us to solve it". He went on to stress
the morals to be learned from their study.
Symbolically, their meanings included those
of wisdom and understanding.

ABOVE Globes of the
kind found in many
Masonic lodges in the
early nineteenth century.
They were always
paired – one celestial
and one terrestrial.

THE MOSAIC PAVEMENT

THE PAVEMENT IS ONE OF THE THREE ORNAMENTS OF A MASONIC LODGE, ALONG WITH THE BLAZING STAR AND THE INDENTED TESSEL. THE PAVEMENT ITSELF CONSISTS OF AN INLAID PATTERN OF ALTERNATING SMALL BLACK AND WHITE SQUARES TO SUGGEST THE DUALISTIC ELEMENTS OF DAY AND NIGHT. VIEWS AS TO THE PAVEMENT'S DEEPER SYMBOLIC SIGNIFICANCE DIFFER — SOME BELIEVE, THAT IT IS EMBLEMATIC OF HUMAN LIFE, OTHERS THAT IT REPRESENTS THE TWO SIDES OF EVERYTHING, SUCH AS BLACK AND WHITE, ACTIVE AND PASSIVE, OR EASY AND DIFFICULT.

In Freemasonry the Mosaic Pavement is first and foremost a representation of the ground floor of King Solomon's Temple. Attempts have been made to trace its origins back to the time of the ancient Egyptians. In the *Mysteries of Freemasonry*, for instance, the term "mosaic" is said to be derived from the Egyptian word meaning "saved or disengaged from the waters", which was used to describe the nine months of the year during which the Nile was not in flood. The variegated appearance of the land during the early part of this season, with fields of grain intersected at regular intervals by irrigation canals, was reproduced in temple architecture by the tessellated pavement and the same word was naturally used to describe it.

INTERPRETING THE SYMBOLISM

In Masonic parlance, the Mosaic Pavement is termed "the beautiful floor" of the lodge, the border is "the skirtwork", and the Blazing Star is "the glory in the centre". The Pavement itself is said to represent the earthly aspects of mankind's existence and the trials and tribulations of everyday life. It is called "beautiful" because it is variegated and chequered in colour and design as a reminder of the eternal sequence of day and

LEFT A depiction of an early temple, with plenty of Masonic imagery surrounding the entrance and an early variation of the Masonic Pavement.

night as well as the varied nature of the objects
that decorate and adorn Creation as a whole.

Various interpretations have been put forward
to explain the Pavement's undoubted symbolism.
Some say that it symbolizes "the chequered life
of man" and some that it "represents a life made
up of good and evil". Others hold that it shows
"the joys and sorrows of life". Perhaps the best
explanation is that it is a synthesis of opposites.

THE INDENTED TESSEL
The tessellated border or skirting that surrounds
the Mosiac Pavement is called the Indented
Tessel. This border, according to Masonic
commentaries, symbolizes "those blessings and
comforts that surround us and that we hope
to obtain by a faithful reliance on Divine
Providence, which is hieroglyphically represented
by the Blazing Star in the centre".

In what is termed its lesser aspect, the Indented
Tessel refers to the planets in their orbits around
the sun, but in its more important aspect, it refers
to the canopy of stars that surrounds the universe.
What the symbolism stresses is the inherent
insignificance of humanity unless guided by the
strength and wisdom of the Supreme Being.

INTERPRETING THE SQUARES

Explanations of what the Mosaic Pavement
symbolizes vary. The standard view is that it is
emblematic of human life, chequered with good
and evil. Others hold the view that the squares
represent day and night.

ABOVE This Tracing
Board shows the Mosaic
Pavement and the idea
of progress towards
eventual enlightenment.

ABOVE TOP LEFT This
Tracing Board shows the
Mosaic Pavement with
the two pillars of the
Temple in the foreground.

STAIRS AND LADDERS

PLAYING A MAJOR ROLE IN THE RITUALS THAT ACCOMPANY ADMISSION TO THE SECOND DEGREE, THE WINDING STAIRCASE REPRESENTS MAN'S INSTINCTS TO RISE, EXCEL AND EXPLORE THE UNKNOWN. CLIMBING THE STAIRCASE, IT IS SAID, MARKS HIS PROGRESS ALONG THE SPIRITUAL PATH AS HE EXPANDS AND FINDS OUT HOW TO MAKE FULL USE OF HIS INTELLECTUAL FACULTIES. JACOB'S LADDER FEATURES IN THE FIRST DEGREE INITIATION CEREMONY. IT SYMBOLIZES THE LESSONS LEARNED IN LIFE, WHICH, IF PROPERLY EMPLOYED, INCREASE THE SUM OF OUR KNOWLEDGE. THE LADDER DERIVES ITS NAME AND SYMBOLISM FROM JACOB'S VISION OF A LADDER LEADING UPWARDS TO HEAVEN, AS RELATED IN GENESIS.

RIGHT A late eighteenth-century Irish silver jewel. In most of the Ancient Mysteries, the ladder was a symbol of advancement.

BELOW In this Second Degree Tracing Board, the ladder has become a winding stairway leading to the inner sanctum of the Masonic Temple.

OPPOSITE In the Bible, a weary Jacob lays down and dreams of a ladder or stairway reaching to Heaven. In Freemasonry both the rungs and the whole are symbolic.

For a Fellow Craft candidate, the Winding Staircase is a sign that it is time to embark on the search for divine truth. As he ascends the stairs, he makes two pauses. During the first of these, he learns about the "peculiar organization" of the Masonic Order. This is intended to remind the initiate of the union of men in society, the blessings of civilization and the fruits of virtue. When he pauses for the second time, he receives instruction about the human senses and architecture. The former symbolize intellectual cultivation, while the latter reminds him of the need to cultivate practical knowledge.

According to Masonic teaching, the initiate is embarking on the tortuous climb toward the goal of achievement. No one can see in advance what lies at the top of a winding staircase – the climb must be completed in order to discover it. Hence, there is also the challenge of the unknown to be conquered.

JACOB'S LADDER

Probably introduced into Speculative Freemasonry in the mid-eighteenth century in England (the ladder does not feature in Continental Masonry), Jacob's Ladder may have come from Hermeticism, in which it was a familiar symbol. The steps each have a meaning – the first symbolizes Justice, the second Equality, the third Kindness, the fourth Good Faith, the Fifth Labour, the sixth Patience and the seventh Intelligence. Another interpretation is that they represent Justice, Charity, Innocence, Sweetness, Faith, Firmness and Truth. Taken as a whole, the symbolism seems to point to the connection between faith and heaven, or, as it is declared in Masonic teaching, "Faith in God, Charity to All Men and Hope in Immortality."

JACOB'S DREAM

In his dream of a ladder connecting Earth with Heaven, God promised Jacob his protection and confirmed his pledge to Abraham that the chosen people would possess the whole of the land from the Euphrates River to the south-west. Jacob commemorated the dream by setting up as a monument the stone on which he had rested his head, pouring oil over it to mark the place where he knew that God was present.

In Freemasonry, the ladder always has seven rungs, each representing a particular theological or social virtue. Other ladders also feature in the additional Degrees of the Craft. One, symbolizing the trials and agonies suffered by Jesus Christ, is ascended in the search for the Lost Word. Another mysterious ladder refers to a Mason's moral duties to God, his fellows and humanity as a whole, while a third prescribes the seven liberal arts and sciences all Masons are bound to pursue.

There are two explanations as to why there is an odd number of steps. According to the Roman architect and writer Vitruvius, most ancient temples had odd-numbered steps. The notion was that anyone climbing them would necessarily arrive at the top with the same foot as the one they had started with at the bottom. This was considered to be a good omen. It could also be because, in the Pythagorean system, odd numbers were thought to be more perfect than even ones, so the use of odd-numbered steps symbolized the state of perfection an initiate to the First Degree was expected to attain.

RIGHT Irish Masonic jewels. The ladders shown represent faith in God, charity and the hope of immortality.

BELOW The Degrees of Freemasonry, from an Entered Apprentice at the bottom to the Order of the Temple at the top.

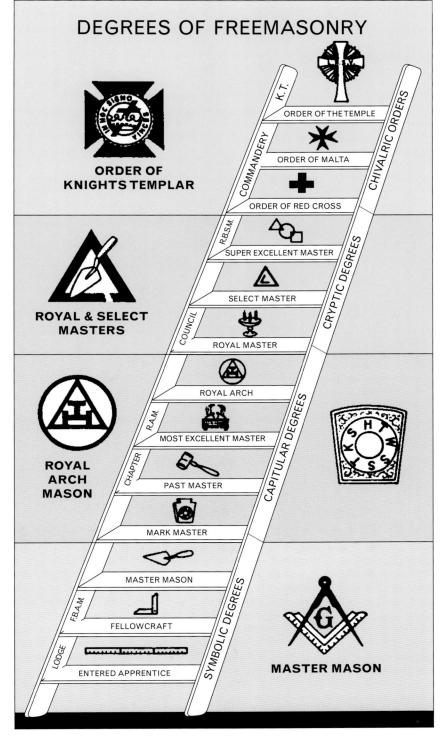

DEGREES OF FREEMASONRY

ORDER OF KNIGHTS TEMPLAR

ROYAL & SELECT MASTERS

ROYAL ARCH MASON

MASTER MASON

K.T. — ORDER OF THE TEMPLE
COMMANDERY — ORDER OF MALTA
ORDER OF RED CROSS — CHIVALRIC ORDERS
R.B.S.M. — SUPER EXCELLENT MASTER
SELECT MASTER — CRYPTIC DEGREES
COUNCIL — ROYAL MASTER
ROYAL ARCH
R.A.M. — MOST EXCELLENT MASTER
PAST MASTER — CAPITULAR DEGREES
CHAPTER — MARK MASTER
MASTER MASON
F.B.A.M. — FELLOWCRAFT
LODGE — ENTERED APPRENTICE — SYMBOLIC DEGREES

THE COFFIN AND SKULL

FOR ANTI-MASONIC POLEMICISTS, THE PRESENCE OF A COFFIN AND A SKULL IN THE SYMBOLIST PANTHEON MORE THAN JUSTIFIES THE CLAIM THAT FREEMASONRY IS BASICALLY UNGODLY AND EVEN SATANIC IN INSPIRATION, HAVING ITS ROOTS IN PAGANISM AND THE OCCULT. WHY, THEY ASK, SHOULD MASONS UTILIZE A SYMBOL WHOSE CLASSIC MEANING, AS IN THE CASE OF THE SKULL AND CROSSBONES, IS DEATH, POISON OR DANGER? WHY WOULD THEY NEED A SYMBOL OF MORTALITY? SUCH VIEWS, HOWEVER, ARE BASED ON A FUNDAMENTAL MISINTERPRETATION OF WHAT FREEMASONRY IS AND WHAT THE MEANING AND PURPOSE OF ITS RITUALS ACTUALLY ARE.

ABOVE The Skull and Crossbones originally made their appearance in French Freemasonry as a symbol of both death and mortality.

Freemasonry is not a religion and promotes no doctrine or dogma as anti-Masonic polemicists would have people believe. The "search for light" is a reference to the Masons' continued quest for knowledge rather than salvation. Though the Craft promotes the hope of resurrection, it does not teach such a belief.

The ritual governing admission to the Third Degree – this is where the Coffin and Skull appear – includes references to the "immortality of the soul", but this is merely a poetical allusion. If anything, Freemasonry teaches that death is a "mysterious veil that the eye of human reason cannot penetrate" and supports the hope, not the promise, of resurrection.

PLACE IN RITUAL

Like many Masonic symbols, the Coffin and the Skull seem to have made their first appearance some time in the eighteenth century. Certainly, the Coffin is depicted on Tracing Boards of the time. It symbolizes death (the skull and crossbones found originally in French Freemasonry has the double symbolism of death and mortality). Their function is to act as symbols during the ritual re-enactment of the murder of Hiram Abif in the rites that accompany initiation into the Third Degree. In them, "the Maul is that by which our Grand Master was slain; the Spade that which dug

RIGHT From *The Perfect Ceremonies of Craft Freemasonry*, 1874, this illustrates the Opening of the Lodge at the beginning of the Third Degree initiation ceremony in which the coffin is prominent.

his grave; the Coffin that which received his lifeless remains; and the Sprig of Acacia that which bloomed at the head of his grave".

According to Harold Waldwin Percival in *Masonry and its Symbols in the Light of 'Thinking and Destiny'*, from 1952, the process starts with an introduction by the Master of the Lodge. Then the initiate's gaze "is directed down in the darkness to an open grave. Inside is a human skull resting on a pair of crossed thighbones." This part of the ritual ends when the candidate is told that "Even in this perishable frame, there resides a vital and immovable principle, which inspires a holy confidence that the Lord of Life will enable us to trample the King of Terrors beneath our feet and lift our eyes to that bright morning star whose rising brings peace and tranquillity to the faithful and obedient of the human race."

THIRD DEGREE LECTURE

The Coffin, Setting Maul (hammer) and Spade all feature in the lecture of the Third Degree. The Maul is "an emblem of those casualties and diseases by which our Earthly existence may be terminated", while the Spade and the Coffin "are striking emblems of morality and afford serious reflection for a thinking mind". The lecture closes with an injunction to "welcome the grim tyrant Death and receive him as a kind messenger sent from our Supreme Grand Master".

The lesson of the legend is not resurrection, however. It is the steadfastness and fidelity of Hiram Abif before his death that is significant, not what happened after it. That is the background to the various secret signs, grips and tokens by which a Master Mason is identified.

LEFT A nineteenth-century Masonic seal showing a skull, crossbones, coffin, and acacia plant.

BELOW A Third Degree Tracing Board helps initiates to understand the significance of the admission ritual.

SWORDS AND DAGGERS

IN THE EIGHTEENTH CENTURY, SWORDS WERE CONSIDERED A PART OF EVERYDAY DRESS — AT LEAST, FOR GENTLEMEN — SO IT IS NOT SURPRISING TO FIND THAT THEY FEATURE IN THE MASONIC RITUALS THAT WERE BEING LAID DOWN DURING THAT PERIOD. TODAY, HOWEVER, THE WEARING OF A SWORD AS PART OF MASONIC DRESS IS CONFINED TO THE ADVANCED DEGREES OF ORDERS SUCH AS THE YORK RITE. IN BLUE LODGE OR SYMBOLIC FREEMASONRY ITS APPEARANCE, EXCEPT AS A SYMBOL, IS PROHIBITED.

As a symbol, the Sword has a classic duality to it. In most cultures, any weapon symbolizes power, but this power can be used in different ways. On the one hand, it can kill and destroy, but on the other, it can protect, defend and counter injustice. This is why swords are often symbolically double-edged. They are also closely linked to light. The Crusaders used to call them "fragments of the Cross of Light".

THE TYLER'S SWORD

Traditionally, the Tyler's Sword should have a wavy blade because it is considered to be a symbol of the flaming sword that, according to Genesis, was placed at the east of the Garden of Eden to protect the Tree of Life. It should never be sheathed as in Freemasonry it is the Tyler's duty to keep all "cowens and eavesdroppers" out of the lodge at all times. It is also a perpetual reminder that nothing unworthy should ever be permitted within the sanctuary of the lodge and the fact that, for every Mason, the Tyler and his drawn sword symbolize the need to be perpetually on guard against the approach of unworthy thoughts and deeds and always remembering the Masonic virtues in the face of enemies. It is also the guardian of the *Book of Constitutions*.

LEFT An elaborately marked Masonic ceremonial sword. Throughout history, swords have been instruments of justice, truth, equality and firmness. They feature symbolically in many Masonic ceremonies.

THE BOOK OF CONSTITUTIONS

Guarded by the Tyler's Sword, the *Book of Constitutions* reminds Masons that they "should be ever watchful and guarded in our thoughts, words and actions, particularly when before the enemies of Masonry, ever bearing in mind those truly Masonic virtues, silence and circumspection."

FAR LEFT In this Masonic medal design, the sword of truth and justice is resting on the altar, directly under the Blazing Star.

THE DAGGER IN RITUAL

Daggers have a specific part to play in Masonic initiation ritual. When a candidate for the First Degree arrives at the lodge, he finds the door guarded by a swordsman, who knocks at the door with the hilt of his drawn sword to ask permission for the candidate to enter. The latter is then hoodwinked – blindfolded – and dressed in a loose-fitting pair of trousers and a white tunic. He wears one slipper, his left leg is bared to the knee, and the left side of the tunic pushed back to expose his left breast. Any metal objects he may be carrying are taken away from him. A hangman's noose is then placed around the candidate's neck and he is led, still blindfold, into the Lodge Room. There, the point of a dagger is pressed to his chest while he undergoes ritual questioning. Once this is over, the dagger point is removed, the candidate kneels, and a prayer is chanted. The initiation ceremony then proceeds through its various other stages, including the customary three perambulations around the lodge, to its conclusion.

BELOW A nineteenth-century First Degree initiation ceremony, in which a dagger is pressed against the candidate's breast while he is being questioned.

GEOMETRIC SHAPES

GIVEN FREEMASONRY'S OBSESSION WITH THE WORK OF PYTHAGORAS AND EUCLID AND WITH GEOMETRY IN GENERAL, IT IS HARDLY SURPRISING THAT GEOMETRIC SHAPES FEATURE PROMINENTLY IN MASONIC SYMBOLISM. MASONS HAVE ALWAYS BELIEVED THAT THE CRAFT AND GEOMETRY ARE INTERTWINED AND THAT A PROPER UNDERSTANDING OF THE LATTER PROVIDES THE MEANS TO AN UNDERSTANDING OF THE FORMER. THIS BELIEF GOES BACK AT LEAST TO THE DAYS OF THE OLD CHARGES. A DOCUMENT DATED 1583 STATES THAT GEOMETRY "TEACHETH A NAB THE METT AND MEASURE OF EARTH AND ALL OTHER THINGS".

Much later, the Masonic authority Thomas Smith Webb was to write: "Geometry, the first and noblest of the sciences, is the basis on which the superstructure of Freemasonry is erected. By Geometry, we may curiously trace Nature through her various windings to her most concealed recesses. By it, we discover the power, the wisdom and the goodness of the Grand Artificer of the Universe and view with delight the proportions that connect this vast machine."

BELOW This eighteenth-century image includes a reference to Pythagoras' theorem at its centre.

THE RECTANGLE

One of the most significant elements of the Tracing Board is the enclosing rectangle, whose proportions follow the precepts of the "golden section" to the letter, and is one of the key features of geometry as originated by the Pythagorean school. At its simplest, the golden section, or ratio, is a simple rectangle whose proportions represent a mathematical sequence.

THE TRIANGLE

In Masonry a triangle can be formed out of the three Hebrew characters "He" or the three 5s. The symbol has several possible interpretations, the first of which is mystical. From ancient times, the equilateral triangle was an emblem of God and a symbol of perfection, which can be attained only by passing through the Valley of the Shadow of Death. This is why the apex of the triangle points downwards. Similarly, the sum of the three "Hes" forming the triangle is 15, considered a sacred number that symbolizes the name of God.

The temporal interpretation relates to the individual in his natural environment and his civic obligations and duties. The first character in the triangle represents the five elements – earth, air, water, fire and the ether. The second represents the five senses and the third concerns the moral responsibility whereby every Mason has to help fellow Masons in times of trouble and to support

Invention and knowledge did not go hand in hand, however. Not only were there no books in existence — at least, as we understand them — at the time when King Solomon's Temple was built, there is also no scriptural account of Hiram having a wife, daughter or any female relative other than his mother — he is described in the Bible as "a widow's son". Nevertheless, Masons believe that the symbol has a place in their traditions, even if it has romance, rather than fact, behind it.

BEES AND THE BEEHIVE

Having made their appearance in Egyptian, Roman and Christian symbolism, the Bee and the Beehive had more ancient pedigrees before they became part of Freemasonry. In the eighteenth century Freemasonry adopted the beehive as a symbol of industry; bees and beehives also symbolize wisdom, obedience and regeneration. Since then the symbols frequently appear in Masonic illustration. According to Albert G. Mackey's *Encyclopaedia of Freemasonry*, the reasons Masons should "go to the bee and learn how diligent she is and what a noble work she produces" is because "though weak in strength, yet since she values wisdom she prevails".

In the *True Masonic Chart*, as well as being "an emblem of industry", the beehive "teaches us that, as we came into the world rational and intelligent beings, so we should ever be industrious ones, never sitting down contented while our fellow creatures around us are in want, when it is in our power to relieve them without inconvenience to ourselves". The parallel here is the instructions given to a Master Mason as part of the initiation rituals of the Third Degree. These state that a Master Mason "works that he may receive wages, the better to support himself and his family, and contribute to the relief of a worthy, distressed brother, his widow and orphans".

BEEHIVES AND SYMBOLISM

The Beehive has had a place in Egyptian, Roman and Christian symbolism. As a Masonic symbol it teaches us that "Industry is a virtue that should be practised by all created beings, from the highest seraph in the Heavens to the lowest reptile in the dust."

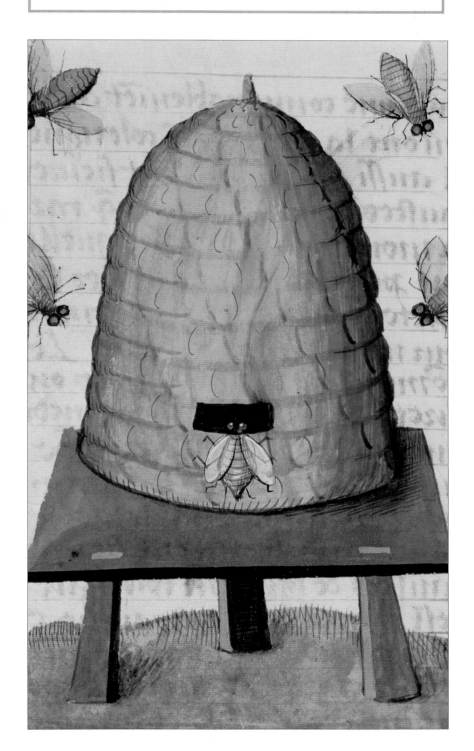

ABOVE Bees returning to the hive. In Freemasonry, the bee is a symbol of industry, obedience and rebirth. It is an appropriate emblem for systematized industry, a virtue taught in the instructions.

LIFE, TIME AND JUSTICE

BOTH THE HOUR GLASS AND THE SCYTHE ARE EMBLEMS THAT FEATURE IN THE RITUALS OF THIRD DEGREE FREEMASONRY, PRIMARILY IN THE UNITED STATES. THE FORMER IS A SYMBOL OF HUMAN LIFE, WHILE THE LATTER IS AN EMBLEM OF TIME, WHICH "CUTS THE BRITTLE THREAD OF LIFE AND LAUNCHES US INTO ETERNITY". TOGETHER, THEY BECOME SYMBOLS OF THE IMPORTANCE OF SPENDING TIME PROFITABLY IN THE SERVICE OF GOD. THE SCALES SYMBOLIZE JUSTICE. THEY ARE INTRODUCED INTO FREEMASONRY IN THE FIRST DEGREE RITUALS, WHERE, ALONG WITH TEMPERANCE, FORTITUDE AND PRUDENCE, THEY FORM THE FOUR CARDINAL VIRTUES.

BELOW The Hour Glass symbolizes human life and its brevity, while the Scythe is an emblem of time and immortality. The message is clear – to make the best use of the time at our disposal.

THE HOUR GLASS

This was probably chosen as the symbol for human life because by its very nature, the Hour Glass is an indication of brevity. Time, so Masonic logic tells us, is the only resource men share in equal abundance. This can be used for fruitful and profitable purposes or it can be squandered. The grains of sand in the Hour Glass pass slowly but surely through it and, before we know it, time is complete. The lesson is that time must be used wisely as time wasted is time lost.

THE SCYTHE

This is a reminder of the certainty of death. While no one can predict when this will be, we must be prepared for an inevitable demise through service to God and to our fellow men. The Scythe is also a symbol of the immortality of the human soul. The unspoken assurance is that, if time is used wisely to acquire knowledge and understanding, which, in turn, is used to serve God and benefit society, then the reward will be great and eternal.

THE SCALES

Justice is one of the Cardinal Virtues. All Freemasons are charged with the necessity of preserving an upright position in all their dealings. This means never failing to act justly in the eyes of their Masonic brethren and those of the world. This is the only cornerstone – another powerful Masonic symbol – on which "a superstructure alike honourable to themselves and to the Fraternity" would be built. This is illustrated in the First Degree rituals, when the candidate for admission is instructed to keep his feet firmly planted on the ground and his body upright.

LEFT A symbol of justice, the scales feature in the rituals governing admission to the First Degree together with the other Cardinal Virtues.

BELOW The crucial stage in a First Degree initiation ceremony when the candidate's blindfold is removed as he stands firmly on the ground.

THE OTHER CARDINAL VIRTUES

The three other virtues are just as clearly defined. Temperance means never revealing the secrets with which an initiate is entrusted through overindulgence – or, as the ritual somewhat quaintly puts it, "in the unguarded hours of dissipation". Fortitude is a reminder that any ills that may befall a person in life must be borne "with becoming resignation". It also teaches a candidate for initiation to let "no dangers or pains dissolve the inviolable fidelity he owed to the trusts reposed in him". The fourth virtue in Freemasonry, Prudence, is considered to be "the true guide to human understanding". In American ritual – the English one differs slightly – it consists of "judging and determining with propriety what is to be said or done on all our occasions, what dangers we should endeavor to avoid, and how to act in all our difficulties".

ORIGINS OF THE VIRTUES

Before at least 1750, there is no reference to the Cardinal Virtues in any Masonic manuscript or ritual. What seems the most likely is that the idea was taken from the Christian church, which itself had derived the notion from the teachings of the Greek philosopher Plato. Freemasonry also borrowed the three Theological Virtues – Faith, Hope and Charity – from Christianity. All of these Virtues feature on the rungs of the Masonic version of Jacob's Ladder.

WHEAT AND PLANTS

IN FREEMASONRY, WHEAT, WINE AND OLIVE OIL ARE SYMBOLS OF NOURISHMENT, REFRESHMENT AND JOY. THEY TEACH MASONS AN IMPORTANT LESSON — ALWAYS TO BE READY TO "NOURISH THE NEEDY, REFRESH THE DESTITUTE AND POUR THE OIL OF JOY INTO THE HEARTS OF THE AFFLICTED". KING SOLOMON GAVE CORN, WINE AND OIL TO THE BUILDERS OF HIS TEMPLE AS A REWARD FOR THEIR LABOURS, WHICH IS WHY, IN THE SECOND DEGREE INITIATION RITUALS, NEWLY ADMITTED FELLOW CRAFT MASONS ARE GIVEN THE SAME "WAGES". PLANTS ARE ALSO IMPORTANT ELEMENTS OF MASONIC SYMBOLISM, NOTABLY THE ACACIA.

THE SYMBOLISM OF WHEAT

The use of wheat (corn) as a religious symbol dates back at least to the time of the ancient Greeks, when it was used as the emblem of the goddess Demeter. In the festivals held in her honour, priests and worshippers alike were crowned with ears of wheat. This symbolized the fertility of the earth, which gave bread to mankind. Thus wheat was the personification of the notions of abundance and fertility. Similarly, wine was the symbol of the Greek god Dionysus, while olive oil was a gift to the Greeks from Athena, the goddess of knowledge. It is the symbol of spiritual enlightenment and peace.

In Biblical symbolism the three products possess a similar meaning and significance, while in Christian liturgy, the corn and the wine are echoed by the elements of the Communion service — the bread and wine represent the body and blood of Christ. The oil is a symbol of baptism. In Freemasonry the grain is the reward given in recognition of the efforts the recipient has made in the building of himself and the temple, the wine is a recognition of his discovery of hidden knowledge and the oil a remembrance of the spiritual enlightenment he has achieved.

A SACRED PLANT

Like the wheat, wine and olive oil, the acacia's role as a significant religious symbol dates back to very ancient times indeed.

In the Bible it is referred to as *shittim* and was revered as the sacred wood from which the Ark of the Covenant was made. In Freemasonry it represents the immortality of the soul — this is how it features in the ritual of the Third Degree in the retelling of the murder of Hiram Abif and at Masonic funerals (though in the latter case, the

BELOW Masonic medals from lodges in Hamburg (right) and Geneva (left) both depict significant symbolic plants.

BELOW RIGHT Wheat has long been associated with Freemasonry. In conjunction with wine and oil they play an important part in the dedication, consecration and constitution of a new lodge.

ABOVE The Square and Compasses with a five-pointed star in the centre. This could be derived from the Star of Hermes, which provided light for travellers along the path to eventual enlightenment.

RIGHT This design from seventeenth-century France is a possible prefiguration of the Royal Arch Jewel.

BELOW RIGHT The Great Magic Circle of Agrippa is based on a six-pointed star, which also appears on Masonic badges.

Masonry. If they did, the fact would surely be at least mentioned in the Old Charges. Additionally, although the Pentagram and the five-pointed star can be interpreted as a representation of the Golden Ratio — which is of substantial importance to Masons — whether the early Freemasons thought of this interpretation is again a matter of controversy.

A SYMBOL OF WISDOM

According to Albert G. Mackey, medieval Freemasons considered the Pentagram to be a symbol of deep wisdom. Its first English mention comes in the legend of Sir Gawain and the Green Knight, where Gawain is described as carrying a shield with "shining gules, with the Pentangle in pure gold depicted thereon". This represented the five wounds of Christ and the five virtues of generosity, fellowship, purity, courtesy and mercy.

THE APRON

ONE OF THE MOST VISIBLE SIGNS OF MASONIC MEMBERSHIP IS THE LAMBSKIN OR WHITE LEATHER APRON — "MORE ANCIENT THAN THE GOLDEN FLEECE OR ROMAN EAGLE, MORE HONOURABLE THAN THE STAR AND GARTER OR ANY OTHER ORDER THAT COULD BE CONFERRED AT THIS OR ANY FUTURE PERIOD" — AS THE WORDS OF THE PRESENTATION RITUAL HAVE IT. IT IS THE PERPETUAL SYMBOL OF MASONIC AFFILIATION. WHATEVER A MASON DOES AND WHEREVER HE GOES, THE APRON SERVES TO REMIND HIM OF HIS MASONIC DUTIES AND OBLIGATIONS. IT IS ALSO A SYMBOLIC REMINDER TO HIM TO DO HIS DUTY TO GOD, HIS COUNTRY, HIS NEIGHBOURS AND HIS FAMILY.

BELOW This nineteenth-century Apron contains a wealth of symbolism, including the Temple of Solomon, the Pyramid, the Cedars of Lebanon, the Pillars of Enoch, the Mosaic Pavement, and various Working Tools.

The origins of the Masonic Apron and its early development and character are obscure. Some trace its roots back to the garb worn by the priests of ancient Egypt, but it is more generally held that the leather apron of the Operative Mason found its way into Speculative Freemasonry together with the Working Tools and other symbols of the Craft. As Masonic rituals developed, so the Apron progressed to the place of prominence it holds in Freemasonry today.

SYMBOLS AND DECORATION

According to W. Kirk MacNulty in *Freemasonry — A Journey through Ritual and Symbol* (1991), "the Masonic Apron was an untrimmed white lambskin tied around the waist. This lambskin had been proclaimed by Masonry to be a badge of innocence and purity."

This proclamation was made some time in the eighteenth century, probably around the same time as the practice of decorating Masonic Aprons with symbolic designs began. In Freemasonry symbols are important elements. The most popular symbols included the All-Seeing Eye, the Columns, and the Square and Compasses. The Apron, which was at first a full-length garment, also became physically smaller. Edgings and other forms of ornamentation began to make their appearance, initially in order to make a clear distinction between the plain Apron of an Entered Apprentice and those of a Fellow Craft and a Master Mason.

THE APRON AS A BADGE

As a badge, the Apron means "membership of the Fraternity" and must always be worn in the lodge. It is the "bond of friendship" and so a symbol of

the brotherly virtues. It is the "badge of
innocence". It "testifies to or witnesses the
honourable age of the Craft". In the Third
Degree it is a badge of authority, which gives a
Master Mason the right to instruct his juniors.

Some Masons have taken the attempt to
discover the significance of all the elements of
the Apron to extremes. They go as far as to argue
that the form of the Apron and the position
of its flap are symbolic. There is little or no
justification for such speculation and the same
goes for attempts to turn the hook (the circle)
and the clasp (the serpent) into significant
symbols. The origins of the tassels and their
seven chains are also shrouded in mystery. Other
decorations are possibly emblematic, but what
they mean is impossible to say.

ABOVE President
George Washington was
a dedicated Mason for
much of his life.

LEFT A Grand Master's
Apron of white lambskin,
the symbol of purity, with
gold. The sun is in the
centre with seven ears of
wheat in each corner.

FAR LEFT This Apron
dates from 1772 and
features an embroidered
triangle. The Apron is an
emblem of innocence as
well as being the badge
of a Freemason.

TRACING BOARDS

INTRODUCED INTO FREEMASONRY IN THE LATE EIGHTEENTH CENTURY AS TRAINING DEVICES, TRACING BOARDS WERE — AND STILL ARE — INTENDED TO HELP CANDIDATES TO MASTER THE INTRICATE SYMBOLISM THAT FEATURES IN THE INITIATION RITUALS FOR EACH OF THE THREE DEGREES. THEIR ORIGINS CAN BE TRACED BACK TO THE DAYS WHEN THE PRACTICE WAS FOR THE MASTER OF THE LODGE TO SKETCH DESIGNS ON THE LODGE FLOOR IN CHALK TO ILLUSTRATE THE POINTS HE WAS MAKING IN HIS LECTURES TO THE BRETHREN. THEN CAME FLOOR CLOTHS AND FINALLY, WHEN LODGES STARTED TO ACQUIRE PERMANENT PREMISES, TRACING BOARDS THEMSELVES.

There are individual Tracing Boards for each of the Degrees. Each board is painted with elaborate emblematic diagrams, featuring the key symbols of the respective Degree, the significance of which it is the Master of the Lodge's task to explain. According to W. Kirk MacNulty in *Freemasonry — A Journey through Ritual and Symbol*, the First Degree Board "sets out the general Western metaphysical scheme" and shows the place of the individual within it. The Second Degree Board is a symbolic representation of the individual in more detail,

BELOW Cypher inscriptions on Harris-type Third Degree Boards with their key. They are used to train Masons in the decoding of the secret parts of Masonic ritual.

while the Third Degree Board "alludes to a process…by which the individual can realize a richer interior potential".

THREE BOARDS, THREE DEGREES

In First Degree ritual, indented borders of black and white triangles surround the Board. The main depiction is of a lodge's interior, the central feature being a Mosaic Pavement of black and white tiles. These, like the other elements shown on the Board, represent duality — light and dark, good and evil, and ease and difficulty. The lodge has no walls and is open to the heavens. This is a symbol of the universal nature of the Craft.

Three pillars — one Corinthian, representing Beauty; one Ionic, for Wisdom; and one Doric, for Strength — stand on the Pavement, together with

Harris-type Third Degree Codes

>L	TC
⊡⊔	MB
⊓⊐⊔	HAB
⌐⌐	AL

| ⊐< |
| ⊔⊡ |
| ⊔⊔⌐ |
| ⊡L |

Key to cypher reading from left to right

A	B	C
D	E	F
G	H	I

J	K	L
M ·	N ·	O
P	Q ·	R

| S |
| T U |
| V |

| W |
| X Y |
| Z |

Key to cypher reading from right to left

L	K	J
O ·	N ·	M
R	Q ·	P

C	B	A
F	E	D
I	H	G

| W |
| Y X |
| Z |

| S |
| U T |
| V |

INTERPRETING THE CYPHERS

These cyphers, written on the Third Degree Boards, are interpreted using the keys in the illustration. The first line TC is made up of the initials of the password, followed by the letters HAB, the contraction of the name of the main figure in the allegory which makes up the Third Degree. Underneath is the year of the great tragedy, A.L. 3000. AL are the initials of the Latin words, *Anne Lucis*, or Year of Light. In this instance, the light is the Light of Creation.

various implements. In the centre, a pedestal supports an Open Book, on which the Square and the Compasses lie. A Ladder reaches upwards to the Blazing Star in the heavens, where the sun, moon, and seven other stars are also depicted. The symbols on the Ladder's rungs represent moral virtues.

The Second Degree Tracing Board shows the interior of King Solomon's Temple, looking towards the inner sanctum. The two pillars represent Jachin and Boaz, the Winding Staircase leading to the Holy of Holies. The River Jordan can be seen in the background with a small waterfall and an ear of growing corn.

The Third Degree Tracing Board has a solid black border. This has a dual meaning – it is a symbol of mourning and a representation of an open grave. The Coffin has an acacia bush near its head, while the interior of King Solomon's Temple is again depicted – this time as a vignette on the Coffin. The emblems of mortality and the Working Tools of a Master Mason and a craftsman are also displayed. Near the head of the Coffin is an inscribed plaque.

ABOVE LEFT The First Degree Tracing Board, includes a Ladder and the three pillars, and describes the place of the human individual in a broad context.

ABOVE MIDDLE The Second Degree Tracing Board shows King Solomon's Temple, in which the individual can ascend a spiral staircase leading to the interior.

ABOVE RIGHT The Third Degree Tracing Board includes a Coffin, which is an analogy of death, whereby the individual will transcend his ordinary life and reach richer things.

LEFT These Viennese Masons in a 1791 illustration are using a Tracing Board as an aid to understanding the symbolism of one of the Degree ceremonies.

GLOSSARY

Acacia

An evergreen shrub which, in Freemasonry, is a symbol of the immortality of the soul.

Age

The time Masons need to serve before they can progress to a higher degree. For an Entered Apprentice, it is three years, for a Fellow Craft Mason five years and for a Master Mason seven years.

Alarm

A signal of someone seeking admission to a lodge. It is given by the Tyler knocking distinctly three times on the door to the lodge room.

Allegiance

A Mason owes allegiance first and foremost to the lodge in which his membership is held and second to the Grand Lodge under which his lodge is chartered. Lodge members swear secret oaths and perform secret rituals swearing allegiance to the lodge and its teachings.

Altar

The centrepiece of the lodge room.

Apron

The "badge of a Mason", the first gift he receives, the first symbol to be explained, and the first tangible evidence of admission into the Craft. It is made from white lambskin, which signifies innocence and the need for purity in life and conduct.

Ark

In Freemasonry, the symbol of the lodge, or a chest containing Masonic Warrants, Jewels and Emblems.

Ashlar

A term used by stonemasons to describe stone as it comes out of a quarry. In the First Degree the Rough Ashlar — the unworked stone — is symbolic of man in his natural state. The Perfect Ashlar symbolizes what he can become through Masonic education.

Beauty

One of the three symbolic supports of the Lodge, represented by the Corinthian column, the Junior Warden, who symbolizes the sun at its meridian, and Hiram Abif, because the beauty and glory of King Solomon's Temple were the result of his skill.

Blue Lodge

The basic Masonic Lodge granting the first Three Degrees. The term "Blue Lodge" has gained more widespread usage in recent times, but "Craft Lodge" is the more usual term in the UK.

Boaz

The name of the left-hand pillar that stood in the porch of King Solomon's Temple.

Book of Constitutions

The rules, regulations and legends of the Craft, compiled by James Anderson and first published in 1723.

Cable Tow

A rope for leading or drawing, which features in the rituals of the Three Degrees.

Cardinal Virtues

Freemasonry has four Cardinal Virtues — Fortitude, Prudence, Temperance and Justice.

Chaos

A symbol of the ignorance and intellectual darkness from which man can be rescued by the light and truth of the Craft.

Clean Hands

An emblem of purity. The white gloves worn during Masonic ceremonies are a direct allusion to the symbol.

Colours

Masonic colours represent the four elements: white symbolizes the earth, purple the sea, sky blue is the air and crimson is fire.

Cornerstone

In Masonic buildings the cornerstone is always placed in the north-east corner. Its surfaces must be square and its solid contents a cube — symbols of morality and truth. Its positioning symbolizes progress from ignorance to knowledge.

Cowan

One of the uninitiated, from who Masonic secrets must be kept.

Darkness to Light

All candidates for the Three Degrees are required to enter the lodge in total darkness as a necessary preliminary to receiving the Light they wish for and seek.

Degree

A grade that prepares a Freemason to go to another higher degree. The first three degrees are Entered Apprentice, Fellow Craft and Master Mason.

East

In Freemasonry the east, where the Master of the Lodge sits, is symbolic of light. Lodge halls and rooms are oblong from east to west, while candidates for the Three Degrees progress from west to east in search of Light.

Five

Among Masons five is a sacred number, second in importance only to three and seven. In the Fellow Craft Degree, for instance, five men are required to hold a lodge, while in the Third Degree, there are references to five points of fellowship and the symbol of the five-pointed star.

Floor Cloth

A framework of board or canvas on which the emblems of any particular degree are inscribed to aid the Master of the Lodge when lecturing.

G

The symbol for God or Geometry. It is usually painted on the east wall of a lodge or sculpted in wood or metal and hung over the Master's chair.

High Twelve

The Masonic term for noon, when members of a lodge are called to take refreshment from their labours.

Jachin

The name of the right-hand column in the porch of King Solomon's Temple. It is

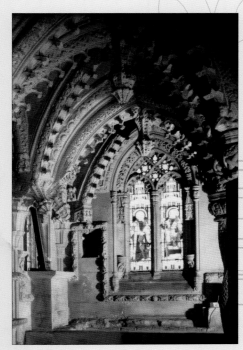

associated with establishment, legality, the Junior Warden and the Fellow Craft.

Jewels

Every Masonic Lodge has six jewels – three Immovable and three Movable. In English Masonry the former are the Square, Level and Plumb Line and the latter the two Ashlars and the Trestle-board. The opposite is the case in American Masonry.

Labyrinth

A symbol of the journey through life.

Landmarks

The most important are the methods of recognition, the government of the Craft and the prerogatives of the Grand Master.

Liberal Arts

The seven arts and sciences decreed worthy of study in Second Degree Freemasonry.

Light

The Lesser Lights are candles placed east, west and south in the lodge, while the Fixed Lights are the windows to the east, west and south. The Three Great Lights are the Volume of Sacred Law, the Square and the Compasses.

Maul

An old name for a mallet.

Oblong Square

A symbol of the lodge, King Solomon's Temple and Noah's Ark.

Pedestals

Substitutes for the three columns of Wisdom, Strength, and Beauty. The three superior officers of the lodge sit at them.

Piece of Architecture

Any work of literature dealing with the Craft.

Serpent

A symbol of wisdom and healing. When depicted with its tail in its mouth, it symbolizes eternity.

So Mote It Be

The Masonic equivalent of Amen.

Tracing Boards

A means of recording the emblems associated with a particular Masonic Degree.

Trestle-board

The board on which the Master of the Lodge draws in a symbolic act representing the building of temples in heart and mind.

Triangle

Equilateral triangles are symbols of perfection; double triangles of deity; and triple triangles, or pentalpha, of health and fellowship.

Tyler

The name of the office of the outer guard of the Freemason's lodge, who guards the door.

Winding Staircase

The way up to the middle chamber of the temple. The steps, spiral and columns have important Masonic significance.

INDEX

Jefferson, Thomas 76
jewels 84–5

K
Kent, William 47
key symbols 84–5
Kilbourne, Hector 77
King Solomon's Temple 9, 11, 16, 35, 36–7, 44, 52–3
Knights Templar 10, 14, 15

L
labyrinths 21, 35, 54
ladders 68–9
Lafayette, Marquis de 27
Langley, Batty 40–1
Le Nôtre, André 76
L'Enfant, Pierre Charles 76
Leo XII, Pope 31
Leo XIII, Pope 31
Lesser Lights 63–4
lettuce 83
Level, the 50, 62, 84, 85
lilies 16
lodges (temples) 19, 42–5
lotus 83

M
Mainz, Archbishop of 60
maps 65
Master Mason initiation 18, 29, 70–1, 82–3
Maurras, Charles 31
mazes *see* labyrinths
Mazzini, Giuseppe 31
Mercury (god) 47
Mesopotamia 18, 86
Minos, King 21
mistletoe 83
Mithraism 19
Molay, Jacques de 14
Moon, the 62–3
Moon Lodges 63

Mosaic Pavement 43, 66–7
Movable Jewels 84, 85
Mozart, Wolfgang Amadeus 12
Mussolini, Benito 31
mystery cults 18–19

N
Napoleon 38
Newton, Isaac 24
noon 18
Norton, Eliot Charles 59

O
obelisks 38, 39, 46
Old Charges 16–17
olive oil 82
Open Book, the 78
Operative Masonry 13, 23, 35
orders of architecture 40
origins 10–11, 14–15
Osiris (god) 16, 18, 20, 44

P
Palladio, Andrea 41
passwords 11
Pennsylvania, Grand Lodge of 26
pentagrams 21, 86–7
Perdix 21
Père-Lachaise, Paris 47
Perfect Ashlar 32, 62, 85
Philip IV, King of France 14
Pike, Albert 44
pillars 16, 56–7
    see also Boaz; Jachin
Plumb, the 50, 62, 84, 85
plumb line, invention of 21
pomegranates 16
Premier Grand Lodge 26, 44, 62
Preston, William 65
Prudence 81
Ptah (god) 55
pyramids 38, 39, 46, 47, 54–5
Pythagoras 21, 40, 69, 74

R
Re (god) 60
Reagan, Ronald 31
Regius Manuscript 17
Renaissance 22–3
Roman Catholic Church 9, 22, 25, 27, 30–1
Rome, Ancient 18, 78

Roosevelt, Franklin Delano 31
Rosslyn Chapel, Scotland 15
rotundas 46
Rough Ashlar 32, 62
Rousseau, Jean-Jacques 46
Royal Arch Degree 28
Royal Arch Halls, Chapter Room, Edinburgh 45
Royal Society, London 24, 25
Russia 26

S
St Clair, Sir William 15
Sandusky, Ohio 77
Schaw, Sir William 22
Scotland 14–15, 22–3, 45, 56
Scottish Rite 28, 44
Scythe, the 80
secrecy 11, 22, 25, 43
Sieyès, Emmanuel-Joseph 27
Silvergate Temple, San Diego 45
Skull, the 70–1
Solomon, King 9, 11, 18, 36, 64
    see also King Solomon's Temple
Speculative Masonry, origins 12, 23, 25, 34, 35
sphinxes 38, 39, 46
Square, the 8, 19, 50, 62, 84, 85
stairs 68–9
star symbols
    Blazing Star 44, 60, 61, 66–7
    five- and seven-pointed 34–5
stonemasons 8–9, 10–11
Stowe, Buckinghamshire 46, 47
Strawberry Hill, Twickenham 46
sun, the 60
Switzerland 26
Sword, the 72

T
Temperance 81
temples *see* lodges
Thoth (god) 20
Three Lights, The 28–9
tools *see* Working Tools
Tracing Boards 90–1
Triangle, the 74–5

Trowel, the 51
24-inch Gauge 50
Tyler's Sword 72

U
United Grand Lodge of England 27
USA 26, 30, 31
    American Revolution 27
    architecture 42, 76–7
    Great Seal 58–9

V
Vanbrugh, Sir John 47
Vitruvius 40, 41

W
Washington, George 12, 27, 76
    Masonic National Memorial 45
Washington DC 76–7
wheat 82
Winding Staircase 68
wine 82
women in Masonry 30
Working Tools 50–1
Wren, Christopher 24, 76

Y
York Rite 28, 72

Z
Zodiac, signs of the 44

BIBLIOGRAPHY

The vast number of books on Freemasonry — "the architecture of the craft" as Masons refer to such writings — is daunting. Some are sensational would-be exposés while others are far better. Here are a few of the more thought-provoking. It is also well worth researching the subject on the internet, as many lodges — particularly in the United States — have informative and helpful websites, while some of the classic Masonic texts, which can be hard to find or are out of print, are now available online.

Baignent, Michael, and Leigh, Richard

The Temple and The Lodge (Arcade Publishing, New York, 1989)

Carr, Harry

The Freemason at Work (Lewis Masonic, Shepperton, 1992)

Coil, James Stevens

Coil's Masonic Encyclopaedia (Anchor Communications, Virginia, 1991)

Cotterell, Maurice M.

The Tutankhamun Prophecies (Hodder Headline, London, 1999)

Curl, James Stevens

The Art & Architecture of Freemasonry (Batsford, London, 1991)

Duncan, Malcolm C.

Duncan's Ritual of Freemasonry (Crown, New York, 1976)

Dyer, Colin

Symbolism in Craft Masonry (Ian Allen, Shepperton, 1986)

Hamill, John

The Craft: A History of English Freemasonry (Lewis Masonic, Shepperton, 1994)

Hamill, John, and Gilbert, Robert

Freemasonry — A Celebration of the Craft (Aquarian Press, London, 1991)

Jacob, Margaret E.

Living the Enlightenment: Freemasonry and Politics in Eighteenth-Century Europe (Oxford University Press Inc., New York, 1992)

Knight, Christopher, and Lomax, Robert

The Hiram Key (HarperCollins, London, 1996)

Knight, Stephen

Brotherhood: The Secret World of the Freemasons (Stein & Day, New York, 1984)

Lenhoff, Eugen

The Freemasons (Lewis Masonic, Shepperton, 1994)

Mackenzie, Kenneth

The Royal Masonic Cyclopaedia (Thoth Publications, Loughborough, 1987)

Mackey, Albert

A History of Freemasonry (Gramercy Books, New York, 2005)

MacNulty, W. Kirk

Freemasonry: A Journey Through Ritual and Symbol (Thames & Hudson, London, 1991)

Macoy, Robert

Dictionary of Freemasonry (Gramercy Books, New York, 1990)

Ridley, Jasper

The Freemasons (Constable & Robinson, London, 2002)

Robinson, John

Born in Blood: The Lost Secrets of Freemasonry (Evans, New York, 1987)

Short, Martin

Inside the Brotherhood (HarperCollins, London, 1995)

Stevenson, David

The Origins of Freemasonry (Cambridge University Press, Cambridge, 1998)

Wilmhurst, W. L.

The Meaning of Masonry (Gramercy Books, New York, 1995).